Contents

Types of Sentences

There are four types of sentences:

- **statement**
- **question**
- **command**
- **exclamation**

A **statement** tells information or ideas. Use a **period** at the end of a statement.

Examples: We are going to the amusement park on Saturday.
More Canadians own cats than dogs.
I thought the movie was exciting, but my sister didn't enjoy it.

A **question** asks something. Use a **question mark** at the end of a question.

Examples: Has anyone seen my math notebook?
Are you sure you remembered to lock the front door?
Is it raining outside?

Many questions begin with the words *who, what, when, where, why,* or *how.*

Examples: What reason did she give for being late?
Who forgot to wipe their feet again?
How did the dog get out of the yard?

A **command** tells someone to do something. Use a **period** at the end of a command.

Examples: Write your name at the top of the test.
Please hang your coat in the closet.
Press the green button to turn on the printer.

A **exclamation** expresses any strong emotion. Use an **exclamation mark** at the end of an exclamation.

Examples: You scared me!
We won the contest!
Don't ever come back here!

Types of Sentences (continued)

Identify the sentence type. Add the correct **punctuation mark** at the end of each sentence. Write the sentence type.

a) The tornado is coming this way

Sentence type: _____

b) How long will it take you to finish your homework

Sentence type: _____

c) Our new neighbours moved in yesterday

Sentence type: _____

d) I love my new puppy so much

Sentence type: _____

e) Fold the laundry after you take it out of the dryer

Sentence type: _____

f) I wonder who left the window open

Sentence type: _____

g) How did the hamster get out of its cage

Sentence type: _____

h) Set the alarm clock so you don't sleep too late

Sentence type: _____

i) It was almost midnight when our plane finally landed

Sentence type: _____

Complete Subjects and Complete Predicates

There are two parts to a sentence. These parts are called the **complete subject** and the **complete predicate**.

Complete Subject

The complete subject contains all the words that tell **who or what** the sentence is about. In the examples below, the complete subject is in bold.

Example: **A small grey mouse** *ran across the floor.*

This sentence is about a mouse. The complete subject contains **all** the words that tell about the mouse.

Example: **The flowers in the garden** *bloom all summer long.*

This sentence is about flowers. The complete subject contains **all** the words that tell about the flowers.

Complete Predicate

The **complete predicate** includes the **verb** and **all** the words that tell about what happened in the sentence. In the examples below, the complete predicate is underlined.

Example: The tall crane <u>lifted a heavy load of bricks</u>.

The verb in this sentence is *lifted*. The other underlined words help to tell about what happened in the sentence.

Example: An avalanche of snow <u>travelled quickly down the mountain</u>.

The verb in this sentence is *travelled*. The other underlined words help to tell about what happened in the sentence.

Every word in a sentence will be part the complete subject **or** part of the complete predicate. In the examples below, the complete subject is in bold, and the complete predicate is underlined.

Examples: **Two young children** <u>chased after the spotted dog</u>.
            Two players on my team <u>hit home runs in our last baseball game</u>.

Canadian Grammar Practice 5 © Chalkboard Publishing

Complete Subjects and Complete Predicates (continued)

1. In each sentence, underline all the words in the **complete subject**.

   a) The blue car drove along the winding road.

   b) A large black spider crawled across the windowsill.

   c) The boy with the broken leg used crutches to walk.

   d) Our friends from England arrived last week.

   e) The slimy slug left a silver trail across the patio stones.

   f) Inky black clouds covered the sky and lightning flashed.

   g) Half the girls in my class have long hair.

   h) A large flock of geese honked loudly as they flew over the house.

   i) A carton of broken eggs leaked on the kitchen counter.

2. In each sentence, underline all the words in the **complete predicate**.

   a) Marty and Janet looked at the full moon last night.

   b) My mother told me about her childhood.

   c) A pack of wolves howled in the distance.

   d) The tired runner decided not to finish the marathon.

   e) Three swans drifted gracefully across the pond.

   f) Most artists started drawing and painting when they were children.

   g) Minnows darted in and out of the pond weeds.

   h) Most children like food better when they help to prepare it.

3. In each sentence, draw a **vertical line** between the **complete subject** and the **complete predicate**.

   Example: My favourite author | writes suspenseful mystery stories.

   a) My friend Nancy is absent today.

   b) The fire destroyed the red barn.

   c) The people on my swim team feel proud of their achievements.

   d) Many of Jake's friends tried out for the volleyball team.

   e) Aunt Mabel writes in her diary every day.

   f) I told everyone about my camping trip.

   g) My neighbour Ricardo let me ride his new bike.

   h) Many construction workers built the new skyscraper.

4. Identify whether the bold part of each sentence is the **complete subject** or the **complete predicate**. Circle *CS* for the complete subject or *CP* for the complete predicate.

   a) My neighbour's cat **gave birth to eight kittens yesterday**.   *CS   CP*

   b) **Tessa's cousin Jimmy** counted 324 coins from his piggy bank.   *CS   CP*

   c) A colourful fall day **was described in vivid detail in the novel**.   *CS   CP*

   d) **The famous artist Vincent Van Gogh** painted a vase full of sunflowers.   *CS   CP*

   e) **A herd of lazy hippos** snoozed in the cool river.   *CS   CP*

   f) A package from Nana **arrived in the mail two days before my birthday**.   *CS   CP*

   g) Rani's long hair **was cut off and donated to make wigs for cancer patients**.   *CS   CP*

   h) **Warm summer breezes** ripple the surface of the pond.   *CS   CP*

Avoiding Sentence Fragments

A **complete sentence** has a complete subject and a complete predicate. A complete sentence tells who or what the subject is, and what the subject does or did. In the example below, the **complete subject** is in bold. The **complete predicate** is underlined.

Example: **This door** *squeaks loudly every time someone opens it.*

A **sentence fragment** is not a complete sentence. A sentence fragment is **missing** a complete subject, a complete predicate, or both. Look at the examples below.

Example: The man in the long black coat.

This is a **sentence fragment**. It contains a complete subject, but it is missing a complete predicate. The sentence fragment does not tell who the man is or what he is doing.

Example: **The man in the long black coat** *is waiting for the bus.*

This is a **complete sentence** because it has a complete subject (in bold) and a complete predicate (underlined).

Example: Ran all the way home without stopping to rest.

This is a **sentence fragment**. It contains a complete predicate, but it is missing a complete subject. The sentence fragment does not tell who ran all the way home.

Example: **My sister** *ran all the way home without stopping to rest.*

This is a **complete sentence** because it has a complete subject (in bold) and a complete predicate (underlined).

Example: Across the meadow and through the woods.

This is a **sentence fragment**. It is missing a complete subject that tells who or what the sentence is about. It is also missing a complete predicate because it does not tell what the subject is doing.

Example: **Two brown mice** *scurried across the meadow and through the woods.*

This is a **complete sentence** because it has a complete subject (in bold) and a complete predicate (underlined).

Remember to check your writing to make sure each sentence contains a **complete subject** and a **complete predicate**. Revise any sentence fragments you find to create complete sentences.

Avoiding Sentence Fragments (continued)

1. The **sentence fragments** below are missing a **complete subject**, a **complete predicate**, or **both**. For each sentence fragment, circle what is missing.

   a) Crept slowly through the long grass in the field.

   complete subject   complete predicate   both are missing

   b) The people at the concert last night.

   complete subject   complete predicate   both are missing

   c) Behind the bookshelf near the window.

   complete subject   complete predicate   both are missing

   d) The boy in the corner with red hair and freckles.

   complete subject   complete predicate   both are missing

   e) As quickly as possible.

   complete subject   complete predicate   both are missing

   f) Suddenly tipped over and crashed to the floor.

   complete subject   complete predicate   both are missing

2. Beside each sentence below, write **CS** if it is a **complete sentence** or **SF** if it is a **sentence fragment**.

   a) Some of the players were nervous before the championship game. _____

   b) Thinking about the long drive back home. _____

   c) The cat meowed. _____

   d) The street where I live. _____

   e) Some cows eating grass in the field. _____

   f) Walked slowly toward the door without looking at anyone. _____

   g) Hamid ran. _____

Combining Sentences

You can join sentences by using the joining words *and* and *but*.

Use *and* to join two sentences that are related. Look at the example below.

Example: The train arrived at the station. Several passengers got off.
The train arrived at the station, **and** *several passengers got off.*

The two sentences above can be joined with *and* because they are related. Both sentences are about what happened at the train station.

The two sentences below cannot be joined with *and* because they are not related.

Example: Ali and I sometimes study together. Ali got a new baseball glove.

Use *but* to join two sentences when the idea in the second sentence **goes against** the idea in the first sentence. Look at the example below.

Example: I wanted to ride my bike to school. The roads were too icy.
I wanted to ride my bike to school, **but** *the roads were too icy.*

When joining sentences, remember to use a **comma before** the joining word.

---

1. Where possible, use *and* or *but* to join the two sentences. If the sentences **cannot** be joined with *and* or *but*, write "Leave as two sentences."

   a) Rita washed the dishes. I put them away.

   _____

   b) The sky was cloudy. Soon the sun came out.

   _____

   c) Our cat is hungry. She is two years old.

   _____

   d) I thought Kyle was asleep. He was awake.

   _____

Combining Sentences (continued)

You can also use the joining words *or* and *so* to join two sentences.

Use *or* to join sentences when there are **two possibilities**, but **only one** will happen.

Example: He can walk to the library. He can ride his bike.
*He can walk to the library, **or** he can ride his bike.*

Use *so* when the idea in the second sentence happens **because of** the idea in the first sentence.

Example: There was deep snow on the ground. I wore my boots to school.
*There was deep snow on the ground, **so** I wore my boots to school.*

Remember to use a **comma before** the joining word.

2. Use *or* or *so* to join the two sentences.

a) I was tired. I went to bed.

_____

b) Kim might win the race. She might come in second.

_____

c) I can help you. You could ask Jeff for help.

_____

d) The sun was shining. I put on sunscreen.

_____

e) Is Travis coming? Is he still sick?

_____

f) The bus was coming. I ran to the bus stop.

_____

10   Canadian Grammar Practice 5 © Chalkboard Publishing

Correcting Run-On Sentences

A **run-on** sentence contains two complete ideas that are **not** correctly joined together. Look at the example below.

Example: I looked out the window I saw a bird.

Notice that "I looked out the window" is a complete idea, and "I saw a bird" is a complete idea. How could you correct this sentence?

You could use **a comma and a joining word** to join the ideas.

Example: I looked out the window, and I saw a bird.

You could **add a period** to make two separate sentences.

Example: I looked out the window. I saw a bird.

Remember that you **cannot** join two complete ideas with just a comma.

Example: I thought I had lost my keys, they were in my pocket.

To correct the sentence, you could **add a joining word** after the comma.

Example: I thought I lost my keys, but they were in my pocket.

You could **add a period** to make two separate sentences.

Example: I thought I lost my keys. They were in my pocket.

You **should not** join two complete ideas by using a joining word and no comma.

Example: Snow was falling so I put on my boots.

When you use a joining word to join two complete ideas, make sure you use a **comma before** the joining word.

Example: Snow was falling, so I put on my boots.

Always check your writing for run-on sentences. Correct any run-on sentences you find.

Remember that you can use a period to make two complete ideas into two separate sentences.

You can also use a comma **and** a joining word such as *and*, *but*, *or*, or *so* to connect two complete ideas in a sentence.

1. For each sentence below, write *RO* if it is a run-on sentence. Put a **check mark** if the sentence is correct.

   a) It is finally spring, and new leaves are growing on the trees. _____

   b) Cyrus caught a big fish, the one I caught was even bigger. _____

   c) The building was on fire and the fire trucks came quickly. _____

   d) The smoke detector wasn't working, so I replaced the battery. _____

   e) Sheila was going to play soccer with us but she hurt her foot. _____

   f) Ivan could take the dog for a walk or Karen might want to do it. _____

2. Show **two** ways to correct each **run-on sentence**. Look at the example.

   Example: We forgot to water the plants, they died.
   We forgot to water the plants. They died.
   We forgot to water the plants, so they died.

   a) I forgot my umbrella, I got wet in the rain.

   _____

   _____

   b) My foot slipped on the ice I didn't fall.

   _____

   _____

   c) I might get up early tomorrow, I might sleep in.

   _____

   _____

Sentences Review Quiz

1. Write the **sentence type** beside each sentence (statement, command, question, or exclamation). Add the **correct punctuation mark** at the end of the sentence.

   a) Do your homework before you watch TV _____

   b) Why don't you want to come with us _____

   c) I wonder if the store is still open _____

   d) Wow, you really scared me _____

   e) Penguins have wings, but they can't fly _____

   f) How did the dog get so dirty _____

   g) Watch out for that big wave _____

   h) Help your sister set the table for dinner _____

2. In each sentence, draw a **vertical line** between the **complete subject** and the **complete predicate**.

   a) The yellow tulips in the garden started blooming last week.

   b) Kenji won three prizes at the county fair.

   c) My favourite author writes exciting mystery novels.

   d) I took my math book out of my backpack.

   e) A beautiful spotted butterfly flew in through the window.

   f) The index in a book helps you find the information you need.

   g) The judges awarded a blue ribbon for the best cherry pie.

   h) A family of ducks lives in the pond behind our house.

3. Beside each sentence below, write **CS** if it is a **complete sentence** or **SF** if it is a **sentence fragment**.

a) A girl with short blonde hair. _____

b) We laughed. _____

c) Ran out the gate and down the driveway. _____

d) He always daydreams. _____

e) Sunny with cloudy periods. _____

f) First out of the gate. _____

g) Rosie barked. _____

4. The **sentence fragments** below are missing a **complete subject**, a **complete predicate**, or **both**. For each sentence fragment, circle **what is missing**.

a) Climbed down the tree as quickly as possible.

   complete subject   complete predicate   both are missing

b) The very last question on the test.

   complete subject   complete predicate   both are missing

c) Back and forth across the rink.

   complete subject   complete predicate   both are missing

d) Never felt so good.

   complete subject   complete predicate   both are missing

e) Around in circles.

   complete subject   complete predicate   both are missing

f) The blond boy on the bus.

   complete subject   complete predicate   both are missing

Sentences Review Quiz (continued)

5. Each sentence below is made from two joined sentences. Write the correct **joining word** (*and, but, or,* or **so**) and add the **correct punctuation**.

a) We wanted to donate all our old clothes to a charity _____ we packed them in a large box.

b) Uncle Joe speaks many languages _____ he doesn't speak Russian.

c) Did the phone ring late last night _____ did I just dream that it rang?

d) It is very cold today _____ I am wearing my winter coat and a hat.

e) The days have been cool _____ it has been very rainy.

f) I don't like video games _____ most of my friends love them.

g) A lot of snow fell last night _____ we got a snow day.

h) I had a headache _____ I had to go to the meeting anyway.

6. Write *RO* if the sentence is a **run-on sentence**. Put a **check mark** if the sentence is correct.

a) We didn't go to the beach, we played baseball instead. _____

b) My dad loves to dance, but my mother hates dancing. _____

c) Rosa made muffins they tasted great! _____

d) The room was too warm so I opened a window. _____

e) Tim waited for an hour but his friend did not show up. _____

f) No one thought it would rain, they did not bring umbrellas. _____

g) A robin built her nest in our tree, and she hatched three chicks. _____

h) We could go to the movies today, or we could go swimming. _____

Common Nouns and Proper Nouns

A **noun** names a person, place, or thing.

A **common noun** names a person, place, or thing that is **not specific**.

A **proper noun** names a **specific** person, place, or thing. Proper nouns always start with **capital letters**. Look at the examples below.

Common Nouns (not specific)	*Proper Nouns (specific)*
month	*February, October*
city	*Toronto, Calgary*
person	*Mr. Cantor, Julia, Aunt Phyllis*

1. Add one **common noun** in each row. The common noun should fit the examples of proper nouns in the same row. The first row is completed for you.

Common Nouns	Examples of Proper Nouns
a) province	*Ontario, Manitoba, Nova Scotia*
b)	*Saturn, Mars, Jupiter*
c)	*Elm Avenue, Riverside Drive*
d)	*Grenville Shoe Store, Bob's Electronics Shop*
e)	*Africa, South America, Asia*
f)	*Atlantic Ocean, Pacific Ocean*
g)	*Germany, China, India*

2. Correct each sentence by making the **proper nouns** start with **capital letters**. Then underline each **common noun**.

a) The man took a train to regina on a rainy day.

b) Did wendy remember to buy jam at westside market?

c) My friend said that neptune is her favourite planet.

d) Sometimes, uncle julio sails his boat on lake huron.

Exploring Proper Nouns

A **proper noun** names a **specific** person, place, or thing.
Proper nouns always start with **capital letters**.

Remember to use capital letters for the types of proper nouns shown below.

Note that the word *the* usually **does not** have a capital letter when it comes before a proper noun. *Example: We were amazed by the beauty of the Grand Canyon.*

Types of Proper Nouns	Examples of Proper Nouns
Names of **countries, provinces,** and **cities**	Alberta, Saskatoon
Names of **holidays**	Labour Day, Valentine's Day
Names of **people** and **pets**	Jennifer, Dr. Silverman, Fluffy, Uncle George, Grandpa
Names of **days of the week** and **months of the year**	Thursday, November
Names of **businesses, organizations,** and **museums**	Free The Children, Royal Ontario Museum
Names of **buildings, bridges,** and **monuments**	Toronto City Hall, Confederation Bridge, National Artillery Monument
Names of **languages**	Spanish, German, Portuguese
Names of **geographical places** and **features**	Banff National Park, the Rocky Mountains

1. Correct the sentences below by making the **proper nouns** start with **capital letters**.

a) Mr. chong drove across the peace bridge when he visited hamilton.

b) My grandparents will teach me to speak russian when they visit next january.

c) On mother's day, we visited the royal tyrell museum in alberta.

d) The rocky mountains stretch from canada to the united states.

e) Some people say english is more difficult to learn than french.

f) Tourists visiting ottawa often go to see the parliament buildings.

g) Students at lakeview school had a bake sale to help the united way raise money.

Spelling Plural Nouns

To make many nouns plural, just add the letter **s**.

Examples: lamp – lamps   gate – gates   paragraph – paragraphs

For nouns that end with **s, x, ch,** or **sh,** add **es**.

Examples: class – classes   fox – foxes   peach – peaches   wish – wishes

For nouns that end with a **consonant + y**, change the **y** to **i** and add **es**.

Examples: butterfly – butterflies   city – cities

For nouns that end with a **vowel + y**, just add **s**.

Examples: valley – valleys   chimney – chimneys

1. Write the **plural form** of each noun.

a) window _____

b) activity _____

c) lunch _____

d) brush _____

e) monkey _____

f) bus _____

g) tax _____

h) journey _____

i) eye _____

j) library _____

k) holiday _____

l) six _____

m) tray _____

n) beach _____

o) family _____

p) address _____

q) dish _____

r) virus _____

s) coach _____

t) island _____

u) berry _____

v) box _____

w) branch _____

x) eyelash _____

Canadian Grammar Practice 5 © Chalkboard Publishing

Spelling Plural Nouns (continued)

For some nouns that end with **o**, add **es**. For other nouns that end with **o**, just add **s**.

Add es

echo – echoes
hero – heroes
potato – potatoes
tomato – tomatoes

Just add s

patio – patios   video – videos
photo – photos   zero – zeros
piano – pianos
radio – radios

For most nouns that end with **f**, change the **f** to a **v** and add **es**. For a few nouns that end with **f**, just add the letter **s**.

Change f to v and add es

elf – elves   shelf – shelves
half – halves   thief – thieves
leaf – leaves   wolf – wolves
loaf – loaves

Just add s

chef – chefs   reef – reefs
chief – chiefs   roof – roofs
cliff – cliffs   sheriff – sheriffs

For some nouns that end with **fe**, change the **f** to a **v** and add **s**. For other nouns that end in **fe**, just add **s**.

Change f to v and add s   knife – knives   life – lives   wife – wives

Just add s   giraffe – giraffes   safe – safes

2. Complete each sentence by writing a **plural noun** shown above.

a) I often spend rainy days watching _____.

b) Biographies tell about the _____ of famous people.

c) We put _____ from our garden in the salad.

d) The store sells _____ and other musical instruments.

e) Police caught the _____ who stole the paintings.

f) A tornado blew the _____ off some houses.

g) The husbands and _____ dressed up for the fancy party.

h) Please pick up two _____ of bread at the grocery store.

Possessive Nouns

A **possessive noun** shows ownership.

Add an **apostrophe + s** to a **singular noun** to show ownership.

Most **plural nouns** end with **s**. Add an **apostrophe after the s** to show ownership.

Examples: The <u>car's</u> tires were flat. (One car has flat tires.)
The <u>cars'</u> tires were flat. (More than one car has flat tires.)

Add an **apostrophe + s** to a **plural noun** that **does not** end with **s**.

Example: We will collect the <u>people's</u> tickets as they enter the auditorium.

1. Rewrite each sentence. Use a **possessive noun** to replace the **underlined words** in each sentence. Check to see if the **underlined noun** is **singular** or **plural**.

a) We heard the shouts <u>of the children</u> from far away.

_____

b) The house <u>that belongs to my neighbours</u> is for sale.

_____

c) The paws <u>of the tiger</u> had very sharp claws.

_____

d) The chirping <u>of the birds</u> woke me up early.

_____

e) Will the teacher <u>of the students</u> give them homework?

_____

f) The laughter <u>of the women</u> echoed down the hallway.

_____

Possessive Nouns (continued)

2. Rewrite each sentence with the correct **possessive noun**. Watch for **singular** and **plural** nouns.

a) The frantic screams of the parrots made everyone cover their ears.

_____

b) The basketball that belongs to the boy bounced onto our lawn.

_____

c) Claws of cats can badly damage the furniture.

_____

d) Instruments belonging to the band sound beautiful when played together.

_____

e) The pages of the book are all tattered.

_____

3. Circle the correct **possessive noun** for each sentence. Check to see if the noun is **plural** or **singular**.

a) (Sunsets' Sunset's) changing colours are a joy to watch.

b) That tall (womans' woman's) umbrella just blew down the street.

c) (Horses' Horse's) tails are good for swatting flies.

d) Half the (team's teams') players are off sick with the flu.

e) The (children's childrens') teacher taught an exciting lesson about pirates today.

f) The (couches' couch's) cushions are getting flat.

Nouns Review Quiz

1. Circle the **correct word** in brackets.

   a) A (common proper) noun names a person, place, or thing that is not specific.

   b) A (common proper) noun names a specific person, place, or thing.

   c) (Common Proper) nouns always start with capital letters.

2. Add one **common noun** in each row. The common noun should fit the examples of proper nouns in the same row. The first row is completed for you.

Common Nouns	Examples of Proper Nouns
a) language	English, Russian, Spanish
b)	Family Day, New Year's Day
c)	April, October, December
d)	King Street, Finch Avenue
e)	Earth, Mercury, Venus

3. Correct each sentence by making the **proper nouns** start with **capital letters**. Then underline each **common noun**.

   a) canadian inventor alexander graham bell invented the telephone.

   b) Call starwell travel agency to buy your ticket to rome.

   c) My cousin jayden is raising money for toronto general hospital.

   d) Next monday is valentine's day, so my sister is making cards for her friends.

   e) Will mr. blackwell try to learn spanish before his trip to spain?

   f) In ontario, wasaga beach is a great place to visit on a hot day.

   g) Every year, labour day is on the first monday in september.

4. In each sentence, circle the **plural noun** that is **spelled correctly**.

a) My little sister has four toy (monkeys monkies) on her bed.

b) We bought two (peachs peaches) and some (blueberrys blueberries).

c) There are six (zeroes zeros) in the numeral for one million.

d) The bakers used sharp (knifes knives) to cut the (loaves loafs) of bread.

e) In the first (paragraphs paragraphes) of the story, the main character makes three (wishes wishs).

f) He put on his (glass's glasses) to read the labels on the (boxes boxs).

g) The busy (chefs chefes) cut up (tomatos tomatoes) and peeled many (potatoes potatos).

h) On hot evenings, people listen to (radioes radios) on their (patioes patios).

i) The reporters took (photos photoes) and (videoes videos) of the two (heros heroes) who rescued the baby.

j) On our camping (trips tripes), we heard (wolfs wolves) howling every night.

k) Everyone sent their best (wishs wishes) for the war (heroes heros) to come home safely.

l) Tiny sand (flies flys) bite people and (dogs doges) on the beach.

m) My neighbour (fixs fixes) people's (pianoes pianos) in his spare time.

n) The (thiefs thieves) nearly got away, but the (sheriffes sheriffs) caught up with them.

o) Mom cut the apples into (halves halfs) for all the (elfs elves) in the Christmas play.

p) My brother is afraid to stand on (rooves roofs), but he's not afraid of (cliffes cliffs).

5. Circle the correct **possessive noun** in each sentence.

   a) Please help me put away the (children's   childrens') toys.

   b) All the (car's   cars') trunks were filled with suitcases.

   c) One (student's   students') notebooks got wet in the rain.

   d) The (men's   mens') wives had known each other for a long time.

   e) My oldest (brother's   brothers') feet are larger than mine.

   f) The (girl's   girls') father said they could stay up late tonight.

   g) This (author's   authors') books have won her many awards.

   h) The (policemen's   policemens') annual dinner and dance is this weekend.

   i) After it emerges from its chrysalis, a (butterflies'   butterfly's) wings unfold slowly.

   j) My grandfather asked me to help him brush the (ponies'   pony's) manes.

   k) Many of the (boys'   boy's) baseball teams had no spaces left.

   l) (Ontarios'   Ontario's) forests are great places to hike and explore.

   m) The (wives'   wife's) club is for women whose husbands are in the armed forces.

   n) A security (guards'   guard's) duties include catching shoplifters.

   o) (Giraffes'   Giraffe's) necks are long enough to reach the leaves at the treetops.

   p) The creepy (spiders'   spider's) web was large and full of dead bugs.

   q) Across the back was written the (boats'   boat's) name: *Queen of Hearts*.

Action Verbs

The **subject** of a sentence is the person or thing that the sentence is about.

An **action verb** is a word that tells what the subject does or did. In the examples below, the subject is underlined and the action verb is in bold.

*Example: <u>My sister</u> **swims** in the lake.*
In this sentence, the verb *swims* tells what the subject (*my sister*) does.

*Example: <u>A large branch</u> **fell** onto our driveway.*
In this sentence, the verb *fell* tells what the subject (*a large branch*) did.

The verbs *swims* and *fell* both express action, so these verbs are action verbs.

---

1. Underline the **action verbs** in the sentences below. **Do not** underline a verb that **does not** express an action.

   a) Fireworks exploded in the night sky.

   b) The teacher asked us questions about the story.

   c) Ali is always tired after hockey practice.

   d) The wind blew leaves off the trees.

   e) Shawna tripped on her way up the stairs.

   f) The car drove right through a red light.

   g) My uncle is a police officer.

   h) The flag flaps high above our heads.

   i) Mr. Phong gave us each an apple.

   j) Mom told me about her tough day at work.

   k) The sun shines brightly on clear days.

   l) The children were happy all day long.

Linking Verbs

A **linking verb** is a verb that does **not** show an action.

Look at the verbs in the sentences below. Notice that these verbs do **not** show an **action** that someone did or is doing.

Examples: The spaghetti **was** tasty.
Orlando **seems** tired today.
Mrs. Gupta **is** a veterinarian.

The verbs in the sentences above are all linking verbs.

What does a linking verb do if it doesn't show action?

1. A linking verb can link the **subject** of the sentence (the person or thing the sentence is about) to an adjective that describes the subject.

   Example: The spaghetti **was** tasty.

   The subject of the sentence is the noun *spaghetti*. The adjective *tasty* describes the subject. The linking verb *was* links the subject to the adjective that describes it.

   Example: Orlando **seems** tired today.

   The subject of the sentence is the proper noun *Orlando*. The adjective *tired* describes the subject. The linking verb *seems* links the subject to the adjective that describes it.

2. A linking verb can link the **subject** of the sentence to a noun that is another name for the subject.

   Example: Mrs. Gupta **is** a veterinarian.

   The subject of the sentence is the proper noun *Mrs. Gupta*. The noun *veterinarian* is another name for the subject. The linking verb *is* links the subject to a noun that is another name for the subject. So *Mrs. Gupta* and *veterinarian* are two nouns that name the same person.

Linking Verbs (continued)

1. The **subject** in each sentence is underlined. The **linking verb** is in bold. Circle the **adjective** that describes the subject **or** the **noun** that is another name for the subject. Then circle the **correct answer** in the next sentence.

a) <u>Leo</u> **was** excited about the party.
The linking verb connects the subject to (an adjective   a noun).

b) My <u>sister</u> **seemed** upset about something.
The linking verb connects the subject to (an adjective   a noun).

c) His <u>uncle</u> **is** a nurse at the hospital.
The linking verb connects the subject to (an adjective   a noun).

d) The <u>students</u> **became** restless right before recess.
The linking verb connects the subject to (an adjective   a noun).

e) My <u>grandmother</u> **was** a dancer many years ago.
The linking verb connects the subject to (an adjective   a noun).

2. Underline the **linking verb** in each sentence.

a) The thunderstorm sounds very close now.

b) This ice cream tastes minty.

c) Our attic is home to many mice.

d) The leftover chicken bones become stock for chicken soup.

e) John seems nervous about meeting his new neighbours.

f) My friend Nami became a great piano player.

g) An earthworm's body feels slimy.

h) The flowers in Mom's garden smell wonderful.

3. Underline the **verb** in each sentence. Circle **AV** if the verb is an action verb that shows what someone or something does or did. Circle **LV** if the verb is a linking verb.

   a) My parents are proud of my achievements. *AV LV*

   b) The children listened to the voice on the radio. *AV LV*

   c) You were very patient with your little brother this morning. *AV LV*

   d) My favourite teacher is the coach of the basketball team. *AV LV*

   e) This milk tastes sour. *AV LV*

   f) My aunt gave me the recipe for this delicious soup. *AV LV*

   g) That young swimmer is a talented athlete. *AV LV*

   h) The old car became rusty over time. *AV LV*

   i) Water leaked through a hole in the roof. *AV LV*

4. Underline the **action verbs**. Circle the **linking verbs.**

   a) The weather looks good for our picnic tomorrow.

   b) When I talked to Tami, she seemed upset about something.

   c) The kitten's fur feels very soft and warm.

   d) Raking leaves on a windy day is a waste of time and effort.

   e) Ken entered his project in the science fair, and was thrilled that he won a ribbon.

   f) Winter seems to stay forever, and summer always leaves too quickly.

   g) Ani left her mittens on the table at the library.

   h) Our dog always whines when we leave for school.

   i) They say that laughter is the best medicine.

The Helping Verbs *Have* and *Has*

Use the **past tense** of a verb to talk about actions that happened in the past.

Examples: I finished   she laughed   they thought

You can use the helping verbs **have** or **has** with the **past tense of a verb** to talk about actions that happened in the past.

Examples: I have finished   she has laughed   they have thought

1. Complete each sentence by using **have** or **has** with the **past tense** of the verb in brackets. Look at the example below.

   Example: My uncle _____ France three times. (visits)
   My uncle <u>has visited</u> France three times.

   a) We _____ all the dirty dishes. (wash)

   b) My little brother _____ his teeth. (brushes)

   c) I _____ all my answers on the test. (check)

   d) That scary movie _____ many children. (frightens)

   e) You _____ me many times in the past. (help)

   f) They _____ all the pieces back together. (glue)

   g) Melissa _____ to help me clean up. (agrees)

   h) It _____ every day. (rains)

   i) We _____ hearing about your trip to China. (enjoy)

   j) The brothers _____ to join our team. (decide)

   k) Mom _____ all my questions. (answers)

   l) People _____ money to the animal shelter. (donate)

   m) Green caterpillars _____ all the leaves on my rose bushes.
      (eat)

Spelling Past Tense Verbs

For many verbs, just add *ed* to make the past tense.

Examples: **Present tense**: Yuki and Ella <u>jump</u> into the swimming pool.
Past tense: Yuki and Ella <u>jumped</u> into the swimming pool.
Past tense with has: Yuki has <u>jumped</u> into the swimming pool.
Past tense with have: Yuki and Ella have <u>jumped</u> into the swimming pool.

If the verb ends with **e**, just add *d*.

Examples: **Present tense**: I <u>tie</u> my shoelaces.
Past tense: I <u>tied</u> my shoelaces.
Present tense: I <u>fill</u> the glass with milk.
Past tense: <u>I filled</u> the glass with milk.

If the verb ends with a **consonant + y**, change the **y** to **i** and add *ed*.

Examples: **Present tense**: Luca and Ken <u>carry</u> the books upstairs.
Past tense: Luca and Ken have <u>carried</u> the books upstairs.

If a **one-syllable** verb ends with a **consonant + vowel + consonant**, and the final consonant is **not w**, **x**, or **y**, double the final consonant and add *ed*.

Examples: **Present tense**: The cars <u>stop</u> at the red light.
Past tense: The cars <u>stopped</u> at the red light.
Present tense: See the horse <u>trot</u> around the ring.
Past tense: The horse <u>trotted</u> around the ring.

Do not double the final consonant for a verb that ends with **one vowel + w, x, or y**.

Examples: **Present tense**: The girls <u>row</u> the boat to the shore.
Past tense: The girls <u>rowed</u> the boat to the shore.
Present tense: The protests <u>delay</u> the construction of the dam.
Present tense: The protests <u>delayed</u> the construction of the dam.

Do not double the final consonant of a verb that **ends with two consonants**.

Examples: **Present tense**: The candles <u>burn</u> brightly this evening.
Past tense: The candles have <u>burned</u> brightly this evening.
Present tense: I <u>lift</u> the garbage pail.
Present tense: I <u>lifted</u> the garbage pail.

Canadian Grammar Practice 5 © Chalkboard Publishing

Spelling Past Tense Verbs (continued)

Do not double the final consonant of a verb that ends with **two vowels and a consonant.**

Examples: **Present tense:** *The students <u>complain</u> about too much homework.*
Past tense: *The students <u>complained</u> about too much homework.*
Present tense: *The scientists <u>look</u> into the microscope.*
Past tense: *The scientists <u>looked</u> into the microscope.*

Write and correctly spell the **past tense** of the verb in brackets.

a) The runner _____ in two races. (compete)

b) I _____ my foot as I listened to the music. (tap)

c) The squirrel _____ up the oak tree. (climb)

d) Mr. Sanchez _____ the guests as they arrived. (greet)

e) Marco has _____ hard for the science test. (study)

f) On her last visit, my aunt _____ with us for ten days. (stay)

g) Have the workers _____ the leaky roof yet? (fix)

h) I _____ the shopping list to the bulletin board. (pin)

i) The teacher has _____ the writing on the chalkboard. (erase)

j) John _____ up for a book on the bookshelf. (reach)

k) Keisha _____ for half an hour every day last week. (jog)

l) I _____ the children to stay away from the train tracks. (warn)

Past Tense of Irregular Verbs

An **irregular verb** does not follow the rules that apply to other verbs. Make sure you use the correct **past tense** of the irregular verbs on this page.

For the verbs in the chart below, notice that the past tense is **the same,** whether or not the helping verb *has* or *have* is used.

Verb	Present Tense	Past Tense with or Without *Has* or *Have*
to bend	bend, bends	bent
to build	build, builds	built
to buy	buy, buys	bought
to catch	catch, catches	caught
to cut	cut, cuts	cut
to feed	feed, feeds	fed
to find	find, finds	found
to pay	pay, pays	paid
to sleep	sleep, sleeps	slept
to understand	understand, understands	understood
to spend	spend, spends	spent

For the verbs in the next chart, notice that **a different form** of the past tense is used with the helping verbs *has* or *have*.

Verb	Present Tense	Past Tense	Past Tense with *Has* or *Have*
to be	am, are, is	was, were	been
to begin	begin, begins	began	begun
to bite	bite, bites	bit	bitten
to break	break, breaks	broke	broken
to come	come, comes	came	come
to drink	drink, drinks	drank	drunk
to drive	drive, drives	drove	driven
to eat	eat, eats	ate	eaten
to know	know, knows	knew	known
to hide	hide, hides	hid	hidden
to give	give, gives	gave	given

Canadian Grammar Practice 5 © Chalkboard Publishing

Past Tense of Irregular Verbs (continued)

Write the correct **past tense** of the verb in brackets.

a) The children have _____ all the orange juice. (drink)

b) Liam has _____ his dog to baseball practice. (bring)

c) I _____ through most of the boring movie. (sleep)

d) We wondered if Dad has _____ Mom the gift yet. (give)

e) She _____ to hum softly to herself. (begin)

f) Mosquitoes have _____ nearly all of the hikers. (bite)

g) My grandmother has _____ three fish so far today. (catch)

h) Winter weather has _____ once again. (come)

i) My little brother _____ a castle with his toy blocks. (build)

j) I have _____ the treasure map in a safe place. (hide)

k) He spoke very quickly, but I _____ what he said. (understand)

l) Carlos walked the dog and _____ the cat. (feed)

m) We have _____ looking for you all afternoon! (be)

n) Let's go for a bike ride after we have _____ dinner. (eat)

o) Mrs. Polanski _____ over to pick up the crying child. (bend)

p) We have _____ down this road many times before. (drive)

q) The thief _____ the stolen jewels. (hide)

r) Earlier this morning, Dad _____ the grass in the backyard. (cut)

s) My parents have _____ your parents for a long time. (know)

Using *Should* and *Could*

Should and *could* are **helping verbs**.

Use *should* when someone is giving **advice** or a **suggestion**.
Example: You <u>should</u> go to bed early if you are very tired.

Use *should* for an action that someone **expects** will happen.
Example: It is a warm day, so the snow <u>should</u> melt quickly.

Use *could* for actions that someone was **able to do in the past**.
Example: When Mr. Thomas was younger, he <u>could</u> jog five kilometres.

Use *could* when <u>talking</u> about a **possibility** or **something that might be true**.
Examples: After school, we <u>could</u> watch a video at my house. (possibility)
Mrs. Rossi <u>could</u> be at work right now. (might be true)

1. Complete each sentence with *should* or *could*. Under the sentence, underline the **reason for your answer**.

a) When she was younger, she _____ swim across the bay.
(advice/suggestion, expected action, ability in the past, possibility/might be true)

b) Paul is never late, so he _____ arrive on time today.
(advice/suggestion, expected action, ability in the past, possibility or might be true)

c) Mom said I _____ look for my scarf on the floor of the closet.
(advice/suggestion, expected action, ability in the past, possibility or might be true)

d) If your nose is running, you _____ have a cold.
(advice/suggestion, expected action, ability in the past, possibility or might be true)

e) The volcano hasn't erupted in years, but it _____ erupt again.
(advice/suggestion, expected action, ability in the past, possibility or might be true)

f) I turned on the heater, so the room _____ warm up soon.
(advice/suggestion, expected action, ability in the past, possibility or might be true)

g) You _____ always tell the truth if you want people to trust you.
(advice/suggestion, expected action, ability in the past, possibility or might be true)

Using *Should* and *Could*

Shouldn't is the contraction of *should not*. *Couldn't* is the contraction of *could not*.

Use *shouldn't* when someone is giving advice or a suggestion about what **not** to do.
Use *shouldn't* for actions that someone expects will **not** happen.

Use *couldn't* for actions that someone was **not** able to do in the past.
Use *couldn't* for something that is **not** possible or probably is **not** true.

2. Complete each sentence with **shouldn't** or **couldn't**.

a) He _____ speak French well before he lived in France.

b) I left home early, so I _____ be late for school.

c) She was home all day, so you _____ have seen her at the mall.

d) He said they _____ go to that movie because it is boring.

e) You ate a big breakfast, so you _____ get hungry before lunch.

f) Bill is very neat, so he _____ be the person who made this mess.

3. Complete each sentence with **should**, **could**, **shouldn't**, or **couldn't**.

a) I am good at math, so I _____ pass the test.

b) The store was closed, so we _____ buy groceries.

c) You _____ be rude to people if you want to make friends.

d) If Eli can't find his pencil case, he _____ have left it at school.

e) She _____ write her name when she was four years old.

f) The questions look easy, so they _____ take long to answer.

g) If you water the plant regularly, it _____ grow well.

h) The joke he told me was so funny, I _____ stop laughing.

Using the Correct Verb Tense

Use **present tense** verbs for actions that happen in the **present**.

Examples: I <u>tell</u> my cousins all about my trip to Utah.
I <u>am telling</u> my cousins all about my trip to Utah.

Use **past tense** verbs for actions that happened in the **past**.

Examples: I <u>told</u> my cousins all about my trip to Utah.
I <u>have told</u> my cousins all about my trip to Utah.
I <u>was telling</u> my cousins all about my trip to Utah when you called.

Use **future tense** verbs for actions that will happen in the **future**.

Example: I <u>will tell</u> my cousins all about my trip to Utah.

1. In each sentence, write the **correct tense** of the verb in brackets. Look for clues that tell you whether the action happens in the present, past, or future.

a) I _____ the dog on a long walk tomorrow. (take)

b) Last week, Leah _____ her ankle while jogging. (sprain)

c) I can't come right now because I _____ a bath. (take)

d) She _____ to school when it suddenly started to rain. (walk)

e) Now I _____ why my brother is angry with me. (understand)

f) Soon these shoes _____ too small for me. (are)

g) The choir _____ two songs at the concert last night. (sing)

h) Dad _____ the grass when the lawnmower broke. (cut)

i) It _____, and I am getting very wet! (rains)

j) I stare at the sky and _____ the clouds go by. (watch)

k) Julio _____ catch with you after he eats his lunch. (play)

l) My cousin's dog _____ with us all next week. (stay)

Canadian Grammar Practice 5 © Chalkboard Publishing

Using the Correct Verb Tense (continued)

It is important to check your writing to make sure you have used the correct verb tenses. In the sentences below, you will practice checking verb tenses.

2. Look at each **underlined verb**. If the verb tense is **correct**, put a **check mark** above the verb. If the verb tense is **incorrect**, write the **correct tense** above the verb.

a) Tia rode her bike to the movie theatre, so she <u>arrives</u> before us.

b) Eduardo <u>cleans</u> the kitchen while I cleaned the bathroom.

c) I went to bed early, and I <u>fell</u> asleep right away.

d) You are going to bed late, so you <u>will be</u> tired tomorrow.

e) I look over at Angela, and she <u>said</u>, "This movie is great!"

f) It will rain tomorrow, but the weather <u>is</u> nice again by Thursday.

g) I <u>will tell</u> him the whole story after we got home from the baseball game.

h) I was cleaning out my desk, and I <u>find</u> the pen I thought I had lost.

i) She <u>gave</u> me five dollars, and I spent it all at the bake sale.

j) After Priya won the race, she <u>says</u> to me, "I can't believe I won!"

k) There <u>is</u> a letter waiting for her after she got home from her trip.

l) Frank <u>will mow</u> the grass for his grandmother last Saturday afternoon.

Verbs Review Quiz

1. Underline the **verb** in each sentence. Circle *AV* is the verb is an **action verb**. Circle *LV* if the verb is a **linking verb**.

   a) The children slid down the water slide at the amusement park. *AV LV*

   b) We often go to the park on Saturday afternoons. *AV LV*

   c) Tasha seems happy with the birthday gift I gave her. *AV LV*

   d) Some of the windows in the old house were broken. *AV LV*

2. The **subject** in each sentence is underlined. The **linking verb** is in bold. Circle the **adjective** that describes the subject **or** the **noun** that is another name for the subject. Then circle the **correct answer** in the next sentence.

   a) My sister **is** captain of her volleyball team.
      The linking verb connects the subject to (an adjective   a noun).

   b) Dad usually **seems** tired after a day at work.
      The linking verb connects the subject to (an adjective   a noun).

   c) The detective **became** suspicious of the woman in the green coat.
      The linking verb connects the subject to (an adjective   a noun).

   d) Neil Armstrong **was** the first astronaut to walk on the moon.
      The linking verb connects the subject to (an adjective   a noun).

   e) The recipes in this cookbook **seem** healthy.
      The linking verb connects the subject to (an adjective   a noun).

   f) The woman next door **will become** the librarian at our school.
      (an adjective   a noun)

   g) Dolphins **were** the first animals I ever read about. (an adjective   a noun)

   h) That fruit salad **looks** delicious! (an adjective   a noun)

3. Complete each sentence by using *have* or *has* with the **past tense** of the verb in brackets.

a) The squirrels _____ to the top of the oak tree. (climbs)

b) My neighbour _____ all the windows in his house. (cleans)

c) The ice cubes _____ in the hot sun. (melt)

d) The scientist _____ a new type of beetle. (discovers)

e) My class _____ money for a new hospital. (raises)

f) My sister and I _____ a cake for Mother's Day. (bakes)

g) No one _____ any of the ugly cookies I made. (eats)

h) Up to today, our class _____ 50 kilograms of food for the food drive. (collects)

i) Grandmother _____ my mother all of her old jewellery. (gives)

4. Write the **past tense** of the verb in brackets. Watch out for verbs that need **spelling changes** and **irregular past tense verbs**.

b) We all _____ that her conclusion was correct. (agree)

c) The children have _____ a large of carton milk today. (drink)

d) Dad _____ the button back onto his shirt. (sew)

e) The author _____ that no one would like her new book. (worry)

f) My stomach hurts because I have _____ too much. (eat)

g) The dog _____ under the bed during the thunderstorm. (stay)

h) We _____ to visit my cousins during our vacation. (plan)

i) Grandpa _____ a lot of time teaching us how to fish. (spend)

Verbs Review Quiz (continued)

5. In each sentence, circle the **correct word** in brackets.

   a) If I get lots of sleep tonight, I (could should) have lots of energy tomorrow.

   b) He (couldn't shouldn't) have walked to the store and back in five minutes.

   c) I don't have much homework, so it (couldn't shouldn't) take me long to finish.

   d) A traffic jam (could should) explain why the bus is so late today.

   e) These lilacs can go on the desk, but they (could should) also go on the kitchen table.

   f) Dinner has been planned very carefully, so nothing (could should) go wrong.

   g) I haven't gone to the dentist in a while, so I (could should) go next week.

   h) How many apples (could should) fit in your lunch box?'

6. In each sentence, write the **correct tense** of the **verb** in brackets.

   a) Mom can't come to the phone because she _____. (sleep)

   b) I _____ on ice when I slipped and fell. (walk)

   c) I didn't do the laundry today, but I _____ it tomorrow. (do)

   d) The dog _____ as the man tries to pet it. (growl)

   e) Don't water the plants because I just _____ them. (water)

   f) We _____ them the good news as soon as they arrive. (tell)

   g) Yesterday, Kathy and I _____ snails for our project. (research)

   h) The snake _____ across the lawn and into the garden every morning. (slither)

   i) At the meeting tomorrow, we _____ the next step we will take. (discuss)

Pronouns and Antecedents

A **pronoun** is a word that takes the place of a **noun**.

Use the pronouns below to take the place of nouns that name **people**:
I   you   he   she   we   they   me   him   her   us   them

Use the pronouns below to take the place of nouns that name **things**:
it   they   them

---

1. Complete each sentence with the correct **pronoun**. The pronoun takes the place of the word or words in brackets.

   a) _____ has become an amazing baseball player. (Angela)

   b) I was sure I had put _____ in my coat pocket. (the keys)

   c) We hope Claire and Anthony can come with _____. (you and me)

   d) _____ will work together on the science project. (Yuki and I)

   e) Are _____ going to come to the concert? (your parents)

   f) My name is Fred. _____ will be your guide on the tour. (Fred)

2. Use a **pronoun** to replace the word or words in brackets below each blank.

   a) I gave _____ to _____ to buy milk at school.
            (the money)   (Tara and John)

   b) _____ is coming to meet _____ tomorrow.
      (Tom)   (my grandparents)

   c) If you have questions, ask _____ or _____.
                   (Leo)   (Anne)

   d) I will give the books to _____ if _____ have not read
             (the twins)   (the twins)

   _____ already.
   (the books)

Pronouns and Antecedents (continued)

An **antecedent** is the word or words that a pronoun replaces.

Example: (The movie) was great because it had a big surprise at the end.

The pronoun it replaces *the movie*. *The movie* is the **antecedent** of the pronoun *it*.

Example: (The batteries) were dead, so Jan replaced them.

The pronoun *them* replaces *the batteries*. *The batteries* is the **antecedent** of the pronoun *them*.

One pronoun can replace **two or more nouns**.

Example: Sometimes my (brother and sister) argue, but they usually get along well.
The antecedent of *they* is *my brother and sister*.

3. Circle the **antecedent** of each underlined pronoun. Draw an arrow from each **underlined pronoun to its antecedent**.

a) Ivan drew a picture, and his mom put it in a frame.

b) Mom said my glasses were dirty, so I cleaned them with a cloth.

c) My best friend is going on vacation, but he will be back in two weeks.

d) Tanya lost her watch, but she found it under her bed.

e) Many birds came to our birdfeeder, and they ate all the seeds in it.

f) The boys made posters for the concert, and they hope many people will come to it.

g) My parents and I love lasagna, and we eat it at least twice a month.

h) Don and Jeff saw Amanda, so they invited her to come along.

i) Juanita and Amit said, "Please tell us if you would like to join our club."

j) The messy drawer was full of wires and cables, so Lianna put them in a box.

k) When my aunt and uncle arrived, Dad said, "It's so nice to see you!"

Using Pronouns to Avoid Repetition

Notice how the bold words are repeated in the sentences below.

*Samireh looked at her **watch**. The **watch** had stopped. **Samireh** thought the battery might be dead.*

Use **pronouns** to avoid repeating the names of people and things in your writing. Here are the same sentences, but pronouns are used to avoid repeating words:

*Samireh looked at her **watch**. **It** had stopped. **She** thought the battery might be dead.*

Rewrite the **underlined** sentences. Use **pronouns** to **avoid repeating** the words in bold.

a) **Gary and Javi** jumped into the pool. The **water** was cold. <u>The water was so cold that Gary and Javi got out right away</u>.

_____

b) **Eva** was listening to a **song**. <u>Eva was sure she had heard the song before</u>.

_____

c) **Tao and I** went to the store to buy **bananas**. <u>Tao and I saw that the bananas were all too green</u>.

_____

d) The **children** had **grapes**. <u>The children said they would share the grapes with me</u>.

_____

e) **Lisa** saw **Ken and me**. <u>Lisa waved at Ken and me</u>.

_____

f) I borrowed this **book** from **Jean**. <u>Please give this book back to Jean</u>.

_____

Choosing Between *I* and *Me*

I and *me* are both pronouns that you can use to replace your own name. Sometimes you might not be sure which pronoun to use in sentences like the examples below. These steps should help you to decide whether to use *I* or *me* in a sentence.

Example 1: Jerry and _____ looked for the missing wallet.

Step 1: Remove the other person or people who come **right before** the word **and** in the sentence. Then remove the word **and**. This will give you a new sentence, and it should be easier to tell which pronoun to use.

Step 2: Insert *I* in the new sentence. Read the sentence aloud, and listen to how it sounds. If it doesn't sound right, try using **me** and read it again.

Original sentence: ~~Jerry and~~ _____ looked for the missing wallet.
New sentence: _____ looked for the missing wallet. (Use *I* or **me**?)
Try both pronouns: *I looked for the missing wallet.* (correct)
                           Me *looked for the missing wallet.* (incorrect)

Step 3: In the original sentence, use the pronoun that worked in the new sentence.

Correct sentence: *Jerry and I looked for the missing wallet.*

Not all sentences are set up the same way. Here is a different example using a question.

Example 2: Will Aunt Lena be surprised to see my brother and _____?

Follow the first two steps to decide which pronoun to use in Example 2.

Correct sentence: *Will Aunt Lena be surprised to see my brother and **me**?*

Original sentence: *Will Aunt Lena be surprised to see* ~~my brother and~~ _____?
New sentence: *Will Aunt Lena be surprised to see* _____? (Use *I* or **me**?)
Try both pronouns: *Will Aunt Lena be surprised to see I?* (incorrect)
                           *Will Aunt Lena be surprised to see **me**?* (incorrect)

Choosing Between *I* and *Me* (continued)

You can use the same steps to decide between *I* or *me* in sentences that use *or* instead of *and*. Look at the example below.

Original sentence: *Will ~~Jana or~~ _____ win the race?*
New sentence: *Will _____ win the race?* (Use *I* or *me*?)
Try both pronouns: *Will I win the race?* (correct)
                                Will me win the race? (incorrect)

Correct sentence: *Will Jana or I win the race?*

1. Complete the following sentences by writing *I* or *me*. Use the steps explained on the previous page to choose the correct pronoun.

   a) Will my sister and _____ ever finish all these chores?

   b) I wonder if she will let Franz and _____ help her look for her cat.

   c) The detective and _____ believe that the man is telling the truth.

   d) "Hurry up, or you'll be late!" Lu and _____ shouted.

   e) The snake slowly slithered toward my friend and _____.

   f) He asked Sam and _____ to walk home with him after school.

   g) My mother and _____ went to the mall to buy some new shoes.

   h) The movie frightened Lionel and _____, but Mary wasn't scared at all.

   i) I hope the play doesn't start before Rachel and _____ get to the theatre.

   j) Don't forget to visit Lev and _____ over the summer holidays.

   k) Kari and _____ stood at the bus stop waiting for James to arrive.

   l) It was so funny when my puppy was jumping all over my sister and _____.

Choosing Between *I* and *Me* (continued)

2. Use the same steps to decide between *I* or *me* in sentences that use **or** instead of **and**.

a) You can return the notebook to Sandra or _____ next week.

b) Miguel or _____ will come to meet you at the train station.

c) Mom is busy, so Harry or _____ will take the muffins to Mrs. Goldman.

d) Please let Tyra or _____ know if you are able to come with us.

e) The neighbour will chose Rick or _____ to mow her lawn this summer.

f) Depending on who gets home first, my sister or _____ always take the dog for a walk after school.

g) Dad will ask Ravi or ___ to help with the grocery shopping this week.

h) Mom said for us to decide whether you or _____ should set the table tonight.

3. Write the pronoun *I* or *me* in each sentence.

a) We can't decide whether you or ___ should have the last apple, so let's split it!

b) Dad wants to take a picture of Carl and ___ dressed up for Halloween.

c) I think my brother will pick you and _____ to join his team for Red Rover.

d) Leo said that Hanna or ___ can open the door when the next guests arrive.

e) For the talent show, Kenny and _____ will play guitar and sing.

f) That big spider is running toward the dog and _____ really fast!

g) Mom said if it starts to rain, you or _____ will have to run out and quickly take down the laundry.

(h) I can't believe the spelling bee has come down to just you and _____ left standing.

Possessive Pronouns

A **possessive pronoun** is a pronoun that shows **ownership.** Use the possessive pronouns below to show ownership.

mine   yours   his   hers   ours   theirs   its

Examples: Her hair is much longer than <u>my hair</u>.
*Her hair is much longer than **mine**.*

Possessive pronouns **do not** use an **apostrophe** to show ownership.

1. Rewrite each sentence. Use a **possessive pronoun** to replace the underlined words.

a) Her cat likes to play, but <u>my uncle's cat</u> sleeps all day.

_____

b) Our neighbour's house is brown, and <u>our house</u> is white.

_____

c) My pen ran out of ink, so may I use <u>your pen</u>?

_____

d) I hung up my coat, but the twins didn't hang up <u>their coats</u>.

_____

e) His store is not very busy, but <u>her store</u> is always busy.

_____

f) We found Leon's baseball cap, but we haven't found <u>my baseball cap</u>.

_____

g) The silly goldfish jumped out of <u>the goldfish's</u> tank again!

_____

Possessive Pronouns (continued)

2. Replace the underlined words with the correct **possessive pronoun**. Rewrite each sentence so it makes sense.

a) I thought this book was <u>my book</u>, but it <u>belongs to my sister</u>.

_____

b) The dog needed to be washed, and <u>the dog's</u> toenails needed trimming.

_____

c) Whose eyes are bluer: <u>my eyes</u> or <u>his eyes</u>?

_____

d) In the mail, two envelopes <u>belonged to us</u> and two <u>belonged to our neighbours</u>.

_____

e) The strong wind caught <u>the man's</u> umbrella and blew it down the street.

_____

f) This caterpillar is cute. Look at all the fuzz on <u>the caterpillar's</u> body!

_____

g) Most of the class got their tests back already, but I'm still waiting for <u>my test</u>.

_____

h) <u>My sister's and my</u> new bedspreads are very pretty.

_____

i) We can't wait to go to Grandma's house to see <u>Grandma's</u> new kittens!

_____

Pronoun–Verb Agreement

The **subject** of an action verb is the person or thing doing the action. In the examples below, the subject is in bold and the action verb is underlined.

Examples: **Maria** <u>feeds</u> *her goldfish every morning.*
The **crane** *slowly* <u>lifts</u> *the heavy load.*
Two **marbles** <u>roll</u> *across the floor.*

The subject of the verb in each sentence above can be replaced by a pronoun. The pronoun becomes the subject of the verb.

Examples: **She** <u>feeds</u> *her goldfish every morning.*
It *slowly* <u>lifts</u> *the heavy load.*
They <u>roll</u> *across the floor.*

When you use a pronoun as the subject of a verb in the present tense, make sure you use the correct form of the verb.

For most action verbs, add **s** to the present tense if the subject is the pronoun **he**, **she**, or **it**. **Do not** add **s** if the subject is **I**, **we**, **you**, or **they**. Look at the examples below.

Add s
She <u>hear**s**</u> *the man shout.*
He <u>run**s**</u> *down the street.*
It <u>fall**s**</u> *to the floor.*
She *quickly* <u>open**s**</u> *the door.*

Do Not Add s
I <u>hear</u> *the man shout.*
We <u>run</u> *down the street.*
They <u>fall</u> *to the floor.*
You *quickly* <u>open</u> *the door.*

For most action verbs that end with **s**, **sh**, **ch**, or **x**, add **es** if the subject is the pronoun **he**, **she**, or **it**.

Example: **She** <u>guess**es**</u> *the answer to the riddle.*

When you use the correct form of the verb with a pronoun, we say that the pronoun and verb "agree."

Note that the verb **have** does not follow the rule of adding **s** when the subject is **he**, **she**, or **it**. This verb has special forms for the present tense.

Examples: **I** <u>have</u> *two quarters in my pocket.*
You <u>have</u> *three sisters.*
He <u>has</u> *a new baseball glove.*
She <u>has</u> *a new watch.*

You *all* <u>have</u> *some homework to do.*
We <u>have</u> *gifts for the children.*
They <u>have</u> *soap to wash their hands.*

Pronoun–Verb Agreement (continued)

1. Circle the correct **verb** in brackets. Make sure that the **pronoun** and **verb** agree.

   a) They (comb combs) their messy hair.

   b) She (answer answers) the question correctly.

   c) He (have has) a scrape on his knee.

   d) We (shout shouts) to our friends on the playground.

   e) They (lift lifts) the chair off the floor.

   f) You (hum hums) a happy tune.

   g) He (show shows) me photos of his family.

   h) It (miss misses) the garbage can, and it (land lands) on the floor.

   i) I (borrow borrows) an eraser from Carly.

   j) They (has have) mud all over their clothes.

2. Write the correct form of the **verb** in brackets to make the **pronoun** and **verb** agree.

   a) It just _____ inside this small box. (fit)

   b) We _____ the flowers in large vases. (arrange)

   c) He often _____ other students in his class. (help)

   d) They sometimes _____ in the park. (play)

   e) She _____ the door that has the broken hinge. (fix)

   f) It _____ a powerful motor inside. (have)

   g) I _____ the rain will stop soon. (hope)

   h) You never _____ me when things go wrong. (blame)

Pronouns Review Quiz

1. Circle the **antecedent** of each underlined pronoun. Draw an arrow from each underlined **pronoun** to its antecedent.

   a) Dad told Alex, "<u>You</u> should always look both ways before crossing the street."

   b) The students studied hard for all the tests, and <u>they</u> got good marks.

   c) Yuki and Sonja like jellybeans, but <u>they</u> don't eat <u>them</u> often.

   d) The boys have some library books, and <u>they</u> will return <u>them</u> tomorrow.

   e) Keisha picked up the fossil so <u>she</u> could add <u>it</u> to her collection.

   f) Frank and Joe saw the windows were dirty, so <u>they</u> washed <u>them</u>.

   g) Angela found the keys her dad had lost, so <u>she</u> gave <u>them</u> to <u>him</u>.

   h) Mr. Jonas hung a painting in his hallway to make <u>it</u> look nicer.

2. Complete each sentence with the correct **pronoun** (*I* or *me*).

   a) The teacher thanked Rachel and _____ for volunteering to help.

   b) My brother and _____ ate pancakes for breakfast this morning.

   c) Kenji likes green apples, but Alberto and _____ like red apples.

   d) Do these gloves belong to Alice or _____?

   e) Joseph was surprised when he saw Dad and _____ at the concert.

   f) Kelly, Gary, or _____ will clean up the mess in the kitchen.

   g) Water from the swimming pool splashed all over Angelia and _____.

   h) Jo invited us all to come over, but Petra and _____ couldn't go.

   i) If you need someone to mail the letter, give it to Walter or _____.

3. Rewrite the underlined sentences. Use **pronouns** to **avoid repeating** the words in bold.

a) **Lin** saw **Julio and Eddie**. <u>Lin invited Julio and Eddie to the party</u>.

_____

b) The **twins** have new **hats**. <u>The hats look very nice on the twins</u>.

_____

c) The **gorillas** were given **a big bunch of bananas**. <u>The gorillas ate all of the bananas</u>.

_____

d) **Anna** hasn't finished her **homework** yet. <u>Anna needs to get back to work on her homework</u>.

_____

_____

4. Rewrite each sentence. Use a **possessive pronoun** to replace the underlined words.

a) Your notebook is green, and <u>my notebook</u> is blue.

_____

b) Bob's cat is white, and <u>their cat</u> is grey.

_____

c) Their team played well, but <u>our team</u> played better.

_____

d) Their house is in the valley, but your house is on the hill.

_____

5. Circle the correct form of the **verb** in brackets to make the **pronoun** and **verb** agree.

   a) We (wait waits) for the bus at the bus stop on the corner.

   b) He (miss misses) his sister when she is away at summer camp.

   c) She (raise raises) her hand to ask a question.

   d) They (collect collects) coins from different countries.

   e) When it (crash crashes) to the floor, they are startled.

   f) You (show shows) the class the beautiful drawing you made.

   g) A butterfly sits on that flower, and it (flutter flutters) its wings sometimes.

   h) I cannot (imagine imagines) how difficult it must be to climb Mount Everest.

6. Write the correct form of the **verb** in brackets to make the **pronoun and verb agree**.

   a) The boy plans to _____ a big treehouse this summer. (build)

   b) Once a month, Tami _____ money to her brother to buy a comic book. (lend)

   c) The two cats _____ taken over the dog's bed. (has)

   d) The race car driver _____ one lap around the track. (complete)

   e) Good listeners _____ the best friends. (make)

   f) Learning to play an instrument _____ lots of practice. (take)

   g) My sister _____ playing that music every evening. (practice)

   h) The brightest rainbows often _____ the darkest storms. (follow)

Adjectives Before and After Nouns

An **adjective** is a word that describes a noun. An adjective can come **before** or **after** the noun it describes. In both examples below, the adjective *beautiful* describes the noun *sunset*.

Before a noun: *We looked at the beautiful sunset.*

After a noun: *The sunset was beautiful.*

1. Circle the **adjective** in each sentence. Underline the **noun** the adjective describes. Draw an arrow from the adjective to the **noun it describes**.

   a) I think I'll wear the striped sweater today.

   b) Give me the clothes that are dirty, and I'll wash them.

   c) If the movie is long, I won't watch it before going to bed.

   d) The man who found the expensive necklace returned it to the owner.

   e) She was brave to chase after the thief as he ran away.

2. Circle the **noun** and underline the **adjective** that describes it.

   a) Our dog was so fluffy after her bath!

   b) It's so exciting to find a surprise package in the mailbox!

   c) The pants looked the right size, but the legs were too long.

   d) In summer, we sometimes get severe thunderstorms.

   e) They say that every cloud has a silver lining.

   f) Jack waded through the slippery mud to cross the shallow stream.

   g) The gowns the women wore were glamorous.

   h) Alice is nervous about speaking in front of an audience.

Adjectives Before and After Nouns (continued)

3. Look for **more than one** adjective in each sentence. Circle each **adjective**, and underline each **noun**.

a) Fierce warriors surrounded the ancient castle.

b) Dad thought the old movie we watched was hilarious.

c) Don't walk over the shiny floor in your muddy boots!

d) We were curious about the new restaurant, so we went there for lunch.

e) A huge spider crawled slowly down the wall beside my bed.

f) After the long hike, my legs were sore and stiff.

g) Red and white balloons decorated the huge auditorium.

4. Look at the list of adjectives below. Read the sentence first. Then write the **adjective** that **fits best**.

silver thirsty peaceful morning hungry gooey frightened summer bravest

a) On a sunny _____ day, my family goes to the park for a picnic.

b) Tiny _____ minnows swim by the shoreline.

c) Even the _____ men were terrified of the bear.

d) No amount of coaxing could make the tiny _____ kitten climb down the tree.

e) The boy was warned not to bother the _____ cat while it was sleeping.

f) The warm _____ sunshine poured into her bedroom.

g) The hikers were _____ and _____ after climbing the mountainside.

h) Jack dropped his pizza slice, and his shoe was covered in _____ melted cheese.

Adjectives Can Describe How Many

An **adjective** describes a noun. Some adjectives answer the question "How many?"
Numbers can be adjectives.

Example: Ted has (three) cats.
Three is an adjective that describes the noun **cats**.

Some adjectives answer the question "How many?" but they **do not** describe exactly
how many.

Example: I have (some) pens.
Some is an adjective that describes the noun **pens**.

---

1. Circle each **adjective** that answers the question "**How many?**" Underline the **noun**
   the adjective describes.

   a) The teacher wrote several questions on the board.

   b) At the end of art class, each student handed in sketches.

   c) We put up posters for the play, but few people came.

   d) I used both hands to cover my eyes.

   e) My two brothers helped me shovel the driveway.

   f) Did you know that all snakes are reptiles?

   g) Most people recycle newspapers and cans.

   h) Hundreds of fans showed up for the concert.

   i) Many children wanted to pat the dog and he got scared.

   j) Ten bundles of newspapers are delivered here every morning.

   k) I saw both raccoons digging up grubs in our backyard.

Adjectives Can Describe How Many (continued)

2. In each set of brackets, there are two **adjectives**. Circle the adjective that **describes how many**.

a) My baby sister was given (cute several) toys for her birthday.

b) (Some Yellowed) pages in the old book were stained.

c) (Damp Four) boxes in the dusty attic were empty.

d) The girls were (happily both) wearing new shoes yesterday.

e) I gave my brother (bags lots) of stamps for his album.

f) There were (no broken) carrots left in the bag, so I bought more.

g) (Every This) person in the room clapped and cheered loudly when the singer finished her song.

h) Dad put up a feeder, and (dozens cousins) of birds came to eat the seeds.

3. Cross out the **adjective** in brackets that **does NOT** describe how many.

a) (Millions Families) of monarch butterflies fly south to Mexico for the winter.

b) Roger ate a (couple box) of muffins for breakfast today.

c) (Every This) step the newborn foal took was a little steadier.

d) (All Angry) people in the world are interesting in their own special way.

e) I asked Kim if she had seen (any brown) rabbits in our backyard this spring.

f) (Most Those) people prefer warm weather instead of cold weather.

g) My little sister chose a party outfit for (each that) doll to wear.

h) Ted's nose was running, but (no dirty) tissues were left in the box.

Demonstrative Adjectives

A demonstrative adjective answers the questions, "Which one?" or "Which ones?" The words *this*, *that, these*, and *those* are demonstrative adjectives.

Use *this* and *that* with singular nouns. Use *these* and *those* with plural nouns. Use *this* and *these* for people or things that are close. Use *that* and *those* for people and things that are farther away.

In the examples below, the demonstrative adjective is in bold, and the noun it describes is underlined.

*The blue shirt is nice, but I like **that** <u>shirt</u> better.*
*Ricardo, please put **these** <u>books</u> back on the shelf.*
***This** <u>movie</u> is better than the movie we watched yesterday.*
*I wonder if **those** <u>gloves</u> on the table are mine.*

Rewrite each sentence, using the correct form of the **demonstrative adjective**.

a) These people over by the tree are my friends.

_____

b) Will one of those keys in my hand open the lock?

_____

c) That box I'm carrying is very heavy.

_____

d) Please leave through this door at the end of the hall.

_____

e) Those socks I'm wearing are very warm.

_____

f) This rainbow in the sky is beautiful.

_____

Using Adjectives to Compare

You can use **adjectives** to **compare** two or more things.

Example: A lion is <u>faster</u> than a horse, but a cheetah is the fastest mammal.

The adjective *faster* compares two mammals. The adjective *fastest* compares all mammals.

Follow the rules below to create **adjectives that compare**.

1. Add *er* to many adjectives to compare **two things**.
   Example: bright – brighter   A lamp is <u>brighter</u> than a candle.

2. Add *est* to many adjectives to compare **more than two things**. Use *the* before the adjective.
   Example: tall – tallest   Kate is the <u>tallest</u> person on my swim team.

3. For adjectives that end with **e**, just add *r* or *st*.
   Example: large – larger – largest

4. For adjectives that end with a **consonant + y**, change the *y* to an *i* and add *er* or *est*.
   Example: funny – funnier – funniest

5. For adjectives that end with a **single vowel + consonant**, double the final consonant and add *er* or *est*.
   Example: big – bigger – biggest

---

1. Change the **adjective** in brackets to make it compare **two things** or **more than two things**. Remember to write *the* before an adjective that ends with *est*.

   a) The green shirt is _____ than the blue shirt. (nice)

   b) This apartment building is _____ building on the street. (tall)

   c) My new quilt is _____ than the one I had before. (pretty)

   d) Tuesday was _____ than Thursday, but Wednesday was

   _____ day last week. (hot)

   e) My bedroom is _____ than my brother's, but my sister's

   bedroom is _____ room in our house. (messy)

Using Adjectives to Compare (continued)

Make sure you use the correct form of these **adjectives that compare**.

Adjective	To Compare Two Things	To Compare More Than Two Things
good	better	best
bad	worse	worst
far	farther	farthest
many or some	more	most

2. Use the correct form of the **adjective** in brackets. Write *the* before an adjective that compares **more than two things**.

a) The soup he made yesterday was _____ than the soup he made last week. (good)

b) Darnell is _____ batter of all the players on our baseball team. (good)

c) Gina's house is _____ from the library than your house is. (far)

d) The sequel to the movie was _____ than the original movie. (bad)

e) All the malls in our city have lots of stores, but Crestview Mall has

_____ stores. (many)

f) Go past these doors, and you will see that the washroom is _____ door at the end of the hall. (far)

g) Laurie found many seashells, but Jeremy found _____ than she did. (many)

h) This is _____ snowstorm we've had in many years. (bad)

i) I am working harder this year, so I am getting _____ marks than I did last year. (good)

More Ways to Compare with Adjectives

For most adjectives that have **two or more syllables**, we do **not** use the endings *er* and *est* to compare two or more things.

To compare **two things**, add *more* or *less* before the adjective.

*Examples: Brian is **more** <u>helpful</u> than Tammy.*
*This roller coaster is **less** <u>exciting</u> that the last one we went on.*

To compare **more than two things**, add *the most* or *the least* before the adjective.

*Examples: She is **the most** <u>generous</u> person I have ever met.*
*Fred is **the least** <u>confident</u> player on our team.*

In each sentence, circle the correct way to **compare two or more things**. Think about how many things are being compared in each sentence.

a) Elijah's story was (more   the most) imaginative than my story.

b) The purple and green scarf was (less   the least) attractive scarf in the store.

c) An airplane ticket to Texas is (more   the most) expensive than a train ticket.

d) The last comedian told (less   the least) amusing jokes we had ever heard.

e) Ian is (less   the least) careful than John when crossing the street.

f) Maya is (more   the most) honest person I know.

g) A chocolate bar is (less   the least) nutritious than an apple.

h) This is (more   the most) uncomfortable chair I have ever sat in!

i) The new student is (more   the most) cooperative person in our group.

j) I was (more   the most) nervous than Samir before the test.

k) The shouts of the children were (less   the least) annoying than the honking cars.

l) Of all the dogs on our street, mine is (less   the least) obedient.

m) I have lots of mosquito bites, but this one is (more the most) irritating.

Adjectives Review Quiz

1. Circle the **adjectives**. Draw an arrow from each **adjective** to the **noun** it describes.

   a) The man who fixed the roof is very tall.

   b) On sunny days, the children always play outside.

   c) Most dogs like to go for long walks.

   d) Nora put some grapes in the yellow bowl on the table.

   e) The two trees in our backyard are huge.

   f) Several people said the new restaurant is expensive.

   g) The teacher said all assignments must be completed by Thursday.

   h) Tony included several photos in his interesting report.

   i) All children enjoy seeing unusual animals at the zoo.

2. Write the correct **demonstrative adjective** (*this*, *that*, *these*, or *those*) in each sentence.

   a) _____ earrings I'm wearing were a gift from my grandparents.

   b) _____ boat in front of us is large, but _____ boat out on the lake is much bigger.

   c) _____ cloud in the distance looks like a thundercloud.

   d) _____ plants by me have already bloomed, but _____ plants over by the fence won't bloom until next month.

   e) _____ kitten at my feet is very playful, but _____ kittens in the corner are too sleepy.

   f) _____ cushion under my head is soft, but _____ green cushion on the sofa is even softer.

Canadian Grammar Practice 5 © Chalkboard Publishing

Adjectives Review Quiz (continued)

3. Use the correct form of the **adjectives** in brackets. Write *the* before an adjective that **compares more than two things**.

a) Our new air conditioner works _____ than the old one did. (good)

b) There are three hospitals in our city, but Lakeview Hospital is _____ from our house. (far)

c) The cold I have now is _____ than the cold I had last winter. (bad)

d) My friends and I collect rocks. My collection has _____ rocks. (many)

e) That was _____ movie I have ever seen! (bad)

f) Lisa has six cousins, but I have _____ cousins than she has. (many)

g) There are lots of ways to help a friend, but sometimes just being a good listener is

_____ way to help. (good)

4. In each sentence, circle the correct way to **compare two or more things**. Think about how many things are being compared in each sentence.

a) The last question on the test was (more   the most) difficult of all the questions.

b) Miguel and Alexandra were both confused, but Alexandra was (less   the least) confused than Miguel.

c) Both the magician's tricks were amazing, but the last trick was (more   the most) amazing.

d) All the performers in the talent show were talented, but the first performer was (more   the most) talented.

e) There were four types of shampoo at the store, and we decided to buy (less   the least) expensive shampoo.

f) The grey kitten is adorable, but the white kitten is (more   the most) adorable.

Adverbs Can Describe How

An **adverb** describes a **verb**. Some adverbs describe **how** an action happens. Look at the examples below.

Lionel (politely) asked for directions.
The adverb **politely** describes **how** Lionel asked.

The two drivers shouted (angrily) at each other.
The adverb **angrily** describes **how** the drivers shouted.

Not all adverbs end with **ly**. **Well** can be an adverb, but it does not end with **ly**.

Example: He played the piano (well) at the recital.

Don't be fooled by **adjectives** that end with **ly**.

Example: The cat ran away with the smelly (sock.)

1. Circle the **adverbs** that tell how an action happens. Underline the **verb** that each adverb describes. Draw an arrow from each adverb **to the verb it describes**.

   a) The children spoke quietly while their father slept peacefully.

   b) He gently laid the baby in the crib, and then he silently left the room.

   c) I clumsily dropped a dish, which shattered noisily against the floor.

   d) The volcano erupted violently and unexpectedly.

2. Decide whether the underlined adverb describes **how** the action happened. Circle **Yes** or **No**.

   a) We walked to school <u>quickly</u> in the chilly weather.   **Yes   No**

   b) The lonely man had a lovely garden, which he watered <u>daily</u>.   **Yes   No**

   c) Silly Miranda likes fast cars, and she likes to drive <u>fast</u>, too.   **Yes   No**

   d) The lively party ended <u>suddenly</u> when he <u>rudely</u> told everyone to leave.   **Yes   No**

   e) I fell on the ice <u>again</u>, but a friendly person came to help me this time.   **Yes   No**

Adverbs Can Describe When or How Often

An **adverb** describes a **verb**. Some adverbs describe **when** an action happens.

Example: Carlos <u>swam</u> with us (today.)
The adverb **today** describes **when** Carlos swam.

Some adverbs describe **how often** an action happens.

Example: Mrs. Grant <u>jogs</u> (frequently.)
The adverb **frequently** describes **how often** Mrs. Grant jogs.

Circle whether the **underlined** adverb tells **when** or **how often** an action happens.

a) Let's meet <u>later</u> to discuss our plans.   **when   how often**

b) Ingrid <u>sometimes</u> forgets to bring her homework.   **when   how often**

c) We drive to Buffalo <u>occasionally</u>.   **when   how often**

d) Have we met <u>before</u>?   **when   how often**

e) My whole family is going to watch a movie <u>tonight</u>.   **when   how often**

f) She checked the clock <u>constantly</u> while waiting for her date.   **when   how often**

g) Hal had long hair <u>a year ago</u>, but he cut it short <u>last week</u>.   **when   how often**

h) People <u>rarely ever</u> find bits of gold just lying in a creek bed.   **when   how often**

i) The judge will make her decision <u>tomorrow</u>.   **when   how often**

j) We <u>never</u> see bears in these woods.   **when   how often**

k) Tony cleans his room <u>regularly</u>.   **when   how often**

l) <u>Sometimes</u> she forgets, but <u>usually</u> she remembers.   **when   how often**

m) I <u>seldom</u> see Margaret, but I talk to her brother <u>often</u>.   **when   how often**

n) Wanda will read her story <u>now</u>, and you can go <u>next</u>.   **when   how often**

Adverbs Can Describe Where

An **adverb** describes a **verb**. Some adverbs describe **where** an action happens.

Example: The children played outside

The adverb **outside** describes **where** the children played.

Some adverbs describe **where** an action happens, but they **do not** describe **exactly where** it happens.

Examples: anywhere   nowhere

Some adverbs describe a **direction** rather than where an action happens.

Example: When she let go of the balloon, it drifted upward.

The adverb **upward** describes the **direction** in which the balloon drifted.

1. Circle each **adverb** that tells **where** an action happens.

   a) Please sit here during the performance.

   b) We were searching for a mailbox, and we found one nearby.

   c) The grey cat followed us everywhere.

   d) Devin watches old movies downstairs.

   e) A mouse lives somewhere in our house.

   f) The dog slept beside the door all morning.

2. Circle each adverb that tells the **direction** an action happens.

   a) I wonder if ants can walk backward.

   b) This bus travels south on Poplar Road.

   c) The road was blocked, so we could not move forward.

   d) The crowd looked up at the helicopter.

   e) My little sister ran to the left to hide. When I looked for her, she ran to the right.

Exploring Adverbs That Compare

An **adverb** describes a **verb**. Some adverbs **compare** how actions are done. With some short adverbs, you can add *er* to compare **two** actions, and *est* to compare **more than two** actions.

Example: Judy ran fast. Kai ran faster than Judy. Melissa ran the fastest

In each sentence above, the circled adverb describes the verb *ran*.
The adverb *faster* compares **two** actions—how Kai ran and how Judy ran.
The adverb *fastest* compares **more than two** actions—how Judy ran, how Kai ran, and how Melissa ran. Melissa ran the fastest of all three people.

You can use the endings *er* and *est* with the adverb *early*. Change the *y* to an *i* and add *er* or *est*.

Example: early – earlier – earliest

1. Complete each sentence by adding *er* or *est* to the adverb in brackets. Think about how many actions are being compared in each sentence. Remember to write *the* before an adverb that compares **more than two** actions.

   a) My brother, my sister, and I can all jump high, but my brother jumps

   _____. (high)

   b) My little sister walks _____ than I walk. (slow)

   c) The sun shines _____ than the moon. (bright)

   d) Sally sang _____ of all the people in the choir. (loud)

   e) Many people ran in the race, but I ran _____. (slow)

   f) Michael did his homework _____ than Rosa did hers. (fast)

   g) I am taller than Joe, so I can reach _____ than he can. (high)

   h) Mrs. Cortez gets up _____ than Mr. Cortez. (early)

   i) All four people in my family get up early, but I get up _____ (early).

Exploring Adverbs That Compare (continued)

Watch out for the adverbs in the chart below. To make these adverbs compare two or more actions, you need to make some tricky changes.

Adverb	Adverb to Compare Two Actions	Adverb to Compare More Than Two Actions
badly	*worse*	*worst*
far	*farther*	*farthest*
little	*less*	*least*
much	*more*	*most*
well	*better*	*best*

2. Complete each sentence by using the **correct form** of the **adverb** in brackets. Think about how many actions are being compared in each sentence. Remember to write *the* before an adverb that compares **more than two** actions.

a) Ned walks _____ to school than I do. (far)

b) My mom can cook _____ than I can, but my dad cooks

_____ in my family. (well)

c) No one in my group sings well, but Tammy sings _____ than Roger. (badly)

d) Everyone at the party laughed, but Penny laughed _____. (much)

e) Of all the people on my baseball team, Charlie can throw a baseball

_____. (far)

f) We have three dogs, and the smallest dog eats _____. (little)

g) George sleeps a lot, but his sister sleeps _____. (much)

h) It rained _____ here than it did in Montreal. (little)

Canadian Grammar Practice 5 © Chalkboard Publishing

Comparing with *More*, *Most*, *Less*, and *Least*

With many adverbs, we do not use the endings *er* and *est* to compare two or more actions. Instead, we use ***more***, ***most***, ***less***, and ***least***. Look at the examples below.

Adverb	To Compare Two Actions	To Compare More Than Two Actions
carefully	*more carefully* *less carefully*	*the most carefully* *the least carefully*

In each sentence, circle the correct way to **compare the actions** in the sentence.

a) Marco exercises (more   the most) regularly than his brother does.

b) The second witness spoke (less   the least) truthfully than the first witness.

c) The driver in the blue car is (more   the most) reckless of all 12 drivers in the race.

d) The ballerina in the lead role danced (more   the most) gracefully of all the ballerinas who performed.

e) Betty and Rhonda both volunteered to do the laundry, but Betty volunteered (less   the least) eagerly than Rhonda did.

f) All three suspects acted suspiciously, but the first suspect acted (less   the least) suspiciously.

g) We waited a long time for the bus, but my sister waited (more   the most) patiently than I did.

h) All the parents in the audience cheered, but my dad cheered (more   the most) enthusiastically.

i) Everyone in the room donated money to the hospital, but Mrs. Fong donated (more   the most) generously.

j) The youngest lion ate (less   the least) greedily of all the lions in the pack.

Adverbs Can Describe Verbs, Adjectives, and Adverbs

An **adverb** can describe a **verb**. An **adverb** can also describe an **adjective**. Adverbs that describe **adjectives** often answer the question "How?"

Example: My little brother is <u>very</u> shy.

Shy is an adjective that describes the noun **brother**. **Very** is an **adverb** that describes the adjective **shy**. **Very** answers the question "How shy?"

Example: An <u>extremely</u> valuable painting was stolen from the art gallery.

Valuable is an adjective that describes the noun **painting**. **Extremely** is an **adverb** that describes the adjective **valuable**. **Extremely** answers the question "How valuable?"

An **adverb** can also describe another **adverb**.

Example: Shawn walked <u>quite</u> quickly, so he wouldn't be late for school.

Quickly is an adverb that describes the verb **walked**. **Quite** is an adverb that describes the adverb **quickly**. Adverbs that describe other adverbs often answer the question "How?" **Quite** answers the question "How quickly?"

1. Circle each **adverb** that describes an **adjective**. Draw an arrow to the **adjective that the adverb describes**.

   a) Dad was slightly annoyed that I had not cleaned my room.

   b) The roof of our house was badly damaged during the hurricane.

   c) The Hoover Dam is an incredibly huge structure.

   d) Maggie was quite interested in hearing about my trip to Africa.

   e) I thanked the librarian for being so helpful to me.

   f) We didn't swim in the lake because the water was awfully cold.

   g) The children couldn't sleep because they had watched a really scary movie.

   h) The soup was too hot to eat, so we let it cool for a minute.

2. What is the **bold adverb** describing? Circle **V** for a verb, **ADJ** for an adjective, or **ADV** for an adverb.

a) Tim sings **very** well and wants to join the choir. **V ADJ ADV**

b) The error Helen made on her quiz was on a **very** confusing question. **V ADJ ADV**

c) The waiter spoke so **softly** that we could hardly hear him. **V ADJ ADV**

d) People too **often** forget to say "please" and "thank you." **V ADJ ADV**

e) After Hans fell on the sidewalk, his knee had a **slightly** blue spot. **V ADJ ADV**

f) **Quite** suddenly, the heavy rain stopped and the sun came out. **V ADJ ADV**

g) **Rather** surprisingly, I got a perfect mark on the test. **V ADJ ADV**

3. Circle whether the **underlined adverb** describes an **adjective** or **another adverb**.

a) We decided the weather was <u>too</u> hot to go for a hike. **adjective   adverb**

b) I was talking <u>too</u> loudly, so I lowered my voice. **adjective   adverb**

c) The cat looked <u>very</u> curiously at the toy mouse. **adjective   adverb**

d) The socks I liked best were <u>very</u> inexpensive. **adjective   adverb**

e) I could see that my friend was <u>quite</u> upset. **adjective   adverb**

f) He was <u>quite</u> astonished when he won the contest. **adjective   adverb**

g) My piano teacher <u>really</u> enjoyed my performance. **adjective   adverb**

h) The hungry dog ate its food <u>really</u> quickly. **adjective   adverb**

i) My cousins were <u>quite</u> thrilled when they met their favourite singer.
    adjective   adverb

j) She talked <u>rather</u> fast, so I had to listen closely. **adjective   adverb**

Adverbs Review Quiz

1. Circle the **adverb** or adverbs in each sentence. Draw an arrow from each adverb to the word it describes.

   a) Suri usually arrives on time, but sometimes she comes late.

   b) The rain soon stopped, and then we played outside.

   c) The noisy crowd was so loud that I covered my ears.

   d) I know I've met him before, but I can't remember his name.

   e) You'll find a lovely park if you go straight down this road.

   f) Mom didn't sleep well because Dad was snoring loudly.

   g) You should leave now if you want to arrive early.

   h) The snow slowly melted as the sun shone brightly.

   i) I had studied hard, so I completed the quiz quickly.

2. Complete the **sentence(s)** after each example sentence.

   a) Are you <u>quite</u> certain that you <u>never</u> tell lies?

      The adverb **quite** describes the (adjective adverb verb) _____.

      The adverb **never** describes the (adjective adverb verb) _____.

   b) We ate <u>fast</u> because we were <u>really</u> hungry.

      The adverb **fast** describes the (adjective adverb verb) _____.

      The adverb **really** describes the (adjective adverb verb) _____.

   c) My grandfather walks <u>so</u> quickly that I can't keep up with him.

      The adverb **so** describes the (adjective adverb verb) _____.

          Canadian Grammar Practice 5 © Chalkboard Publishing

3. Complete each sentence by using the correct form of the **adverb** in brackets. Write *the* before the adverb when necessary.

a) I can run fast, but my sister can run _____. (fast)

b) My brother and sister get up early, but I get up _____. (early)

c) Talia can throw a baseball _____ than Michelle. (far)

d) Of all the people in my class, Rob talks _____. (loud)

e) I read three books, and the one about whales was _____ interesting. (less)

f) Jodie plays piano _____ than her brother. (well)

g) Most of the plants in my vegetable garden are growing quickly, but the carrots

   have grown _____. (little)

4. Circle the correct way to **compare the actions** in the sentence.

a) Ricardo washes his hands (more the most) carefully than I do.

b) Of the four students who volunteered to stay late, Maria volunteered
   (less the least) enthusiastically.

c) Lucia gets colds (more the most) frequently than her sister does.

d) The knot on my left shoelace was tied (less the least) tightly than the one on my
   right shoe.

e) All three children acted rudely, but Sami acted (more the most) rudely.

f) When the students in our class gave their speeches, Elizabeth spoke
   (less the least) confidently.

g) All the stars shone brightly, but the North Star shone (most the most) brightly.

Using Commas in Lists

A sentence can contain a **list**. If the list has **more than two** items, use a **comma** after each item **except** the last item.

Example: We put grapes, bananas, and apples in the bowl.

Each item in a list can be **more than one word**. Use a **comma** after each item **except** the last item.

Example: We walked up the hill, across the field, and down the road on our way home.

1. Add **commas** to the list in each sentence.

   a) Joan would like to visit Portugal Spain and Italy.

   b) The American flag is red white and blue.

   c) Harvey Melinda Frank and Julio are making signs for the bake sale.

   d) Wednesday Thursday and Friday are busy days for me.

   e) Amy wants to compete in a triathlon race that involves swimming cycling and running.

   f) Mike tries to eat healthy foods such as fruit vegetables and grains every day.

2. Add **commas** to these lists that are **more than one word**.

   a) Dad washed the car cut the grass and fed the dog.

   b) The squirrel ran down the tree along the fence and across the lawn.

   c) My sister my brother and I searched everywhere for the cat.

   d) I spend most of my time attending school doing homework and practicing piano.

   e) The nurse said that eating nutritious foods drinking lots of water and getting enough sleep would help me stay healthy.

   f) I want to finish my homework play a video game and read my book before bed.

More Ways to Use Commas

Use a comma after **yes** or **no** when it appears at the **beginning** of a sentence.

Examples: <u>Yes</u>, *you can borrow my calculator.*
<u>No</u>, *I haven't seen Ralph all day.*

If you add a **question** at the end of a sentence, use a comma **before** the question.

Example: Tara watered the garden this morning, <u>didn't she</u>?

When someone is speaking and says the name of the person they are speaking to, use a comma **between** the name and the rest of the sentence.

Examples: "<u>Tony</u>, did you call me?" she asked.
I replied, "I'm pleased to meet you, <u>Mrs. Walker</u>."

When you are writing a list that has **more than two** items, remember that you need to use a **comma** after each item **except** the last item.

1. Add **commas** where necessary to the sentences below.

   a) The children went outside to play didn't they?

   b) "Terry you need to listen more carefully," the teacher said.

   c) "Maybe you can come too John," I suggested.

   d) No I haven't yet returned the books to the library.

   e) Today is Thursday isn't it?

   f) Yes I followed the recipe, but I think I left the cake in the oven too long.

2. In these sentences that list **more than two** items, add **commas** where necessary.

   a) No I haven't done my homework cleaned my room or brushed my teeth.

   b) "Mr. Schwartz do you speak any languages other than English French and Spanish?" I asked.

   c) This coat hat and scarf belong to Penny don't they?

   d) Sal you set out the utensils plates and glasses this morning didn't you?

Punctuating Dialogue

Use **quotation marks** around words that someone is speaking.

Examples: "The laundry should be dry by now," <u>*Dad said*</u>*.*
"I lived in Ireland before I moved here," <u>*explained Rachel*</u>*.*
"We're over here," <u>*called Katie*</u>*.*

The underlined words are called **speaker tags**. A speaker tag tells who is talking. When the speaker tag comes **after** the spoken words, remember to put a comma **before** the **second** quotation mark. See the examples above.

When the speaker tag comes **after** the spoken words, **do not** put a **comma** before the second quotation mark if there is a **question mark** or **exclamation point** at the end of the spoken words.

*Examples: "Can we go to the mall tomorrow**?**" asked Gary.*
*"I'm so happy to see you**!**" exclaimed Aunt Mary.*

If the speaker tag comes **before** the spoken words, put a comma **after** the speaker tag.

*Example: The salesperson said**,** "Jeans are on sale this week."*

Remember to use a **capital letter** for the first spoken word.

---

1. Add **quotation marks** to each sentence below. Add a **comma**, if necessary.

a) We've won the game!   shouted Chris.

b) I hope we have good weather during our vacation   Dad said.

c) I wonder if she noticed that we came in late   whispered Beth.

d) Would you like to look through the telescope?   the scientist asked.

e) The coach said   Now that's what I call teamwork!

f) The crowd shouted   Don't go yet! Sing one more song!

g) My mom said   I think I've seen this movie before.

h) This produce is all organically grown the woman explained.

i) Tomas can you come up and write that on the board for us? the teacher asked.

Punctuating Dialogue (continued)

In your writing, if someone says a long sentence, you can put the speaker tag **in the middle** of the sentence. Look at the example below.

"I know I put my watch in a safe place," said Rick, "but I can't remember where."

If you are putting the speaker tag in the middle of a long spoken sentence, remember to do the following:

• Put **quotation marks** around the **first part** of the spoken sentence **and** the **second part** of the spoken sentence.

• Put a **comma** at the end of the **first part** of the spoken sentence, **before** the second quotation mark.

• Put a **comma** after the **speaker tag**.

• Put a **period**, **question mark**, or **exclamation mark** at the end of the **second part** of the spoken sentence, **before** the last quotation mark.

• Remember that you **do not** need a **capital letter** on the first word of the **second part** of the spoken sentence, since all the spoken words make up one sentence.

2. Add the **correct punctuation** to the sentences below.

a) My baby cried most of the night   said Mrs. Hernandez   and I think it was because she had a fever

b) The woman who lives next door is a doctor   explained Mr. Carson   but she retired several years ago

c) These red roses are pretty   said the gardener   and the pink roses are even prettier

d) It has been snowing all morning   said Rita   so I think I'll need to wear my boots when I go outside this afternoon

e) My parents said you could come to the amusement park with us   said Eddie   but will you be able to get to my house by noon

Punctuation Review Quiz

1. Add the **correct punctuation** to the sentences below.

    a) Are you feeling well enough to go to school today? asked Dad.

    b) Running cycling and swimming are my favourite sports.

    c) No we must not allow more animals to become extinct.

    d) I'll be ready after I get dressed have breakfast and brush my teeth.

    e) You're going to help me with my homework aren't you?

    f) Watch out Maria! shouted her brother Diego.

    g) Hamid asked Next Monday is Labour Day isn't it?

    h) I might be a while said Jeff so don't wait for me.

    i) Yes I'll remember this wonderful day forever.

    j) You fed the dog the cat and the goldfish right? asked Tanya.

2. In the sentences below, add any **missing punctuation** and circle any **incorrect punctuation**. If the sentence is already correct, put a **check mark** beside it.

    a) "You're Hannah's younger sister aren't you?," asked Mr. Kapoor.

    b) Leah said "My red socks, green sweatshirt and blue blouse, are in the dryer"

    c) No pets are ever allowed in this restaurant said the waiter."

    d) Listening to music, reading a book, and talking to friends on the phone are good ways to spend a rainy day, don't you think?

    e) "The reason I asked you to stay late Lucy", explained the teacher "is to tell you how pleased I am with the improvement in your marks."

    f) "Yes Matthew, I realize that cleaning your room, taking out the garbage and putting away your clean laundry are not fun activities" said Dad "but you still need to do them!"

Using *Either* and *Or*

Either and *or* used together make a positive statement about **two** events. They indicate that **one or the other** will happen or did happen.

*Example: Sonya will **either** walk to school **or** ride her bike.*

In this sentence, there are two possible ways that Sonya can go to school, but she will choose only one of the possibilities.

*Example: **Either** Ravi **or** Sana will help Grandma rake the leaves.*

In this sentence, there are two people who can help Grandma rake leaves, but only one of these people will help Grandma.

Rewrite each pair of sentences as **one sentence**. Use *either* and *or* in the new sentence to show that one of the possibilities **will** happen. See the example below.

Example: I might read a book. I might take a nap.
I will either read a book or take a nap.

a) Harold might help me clean up. Jane might help me clean up.

_____

b) They might swim. They might go for a walk.

_____

c) Cai might wash the kitchen floor. Pan might wash the kitchen floor.

_____

d) The woman might cut her hair. The woman might let it grow.

_____

e) The children might play a game. The children might watch a movie.

_____

Using *Neither* and *Nor*

Neither and ***nor*** used together make a negative statement about **two events** or **two things**. They indicate that both **will not** or **did not** happen, or are **not true** or **not real**.

Example: ***Neither*** *Franz* ***nor*** *Irena saw the woman.*

This sentence tells us that Frank did not see the woman, and Irena did not see the woman.

Example: Lynne likes ***neither*** *cake* ***nor*** *ice cream.*

This sentence tells us that Lynne does not like cake, and she does not like ice cream.

You **cannot** use *or* after *neither*. Always use *neither* and *nor* together.

Rewrite each pair of sentences as one sentence. Use ***neither*** and ***nor*** in the new sentence. See the example below.

Example: We did not see Eduardo at the park. We did not see Tina at the park.
       We saw neither Eduardo nor Tina at the park.

a) Mom could not find our hamster. Dad could not find our hamster.

_____

b) The weather was not windy. The weather was not cold.

_____

c) The book was not in my desk. The book was not in my backpack.

_____

d) Priya could not answer the question. Larry could not answer the question.

_____

e) I was not sick. I was not tired.

_____

Using Capital Letters in Titles

Use **capital letters** when you write the title of a book, story, poem, song, or movie.

Rule 1: Use a capital letter for the first letter of all **nouns, pronouns, adjectives, verbs,** and **adverbs.** Most words in a title will be one of these.

Examples: Three Blind Mice   Charlotte's Web

Rule 2: Do not use a capital letter for the first letter in these short words, **unless** they are the **first or last word** in the title:

a   an   and   by   for   in   of   on   the   to   up   with

Examples: Harry Potter and the Goblet of Fire   The Farmer in the Dell

Rule 3: Always use a capital letter for the **first and last words** in a title, no matter what the word is.

Examples: Let the Sunshine In   Polly Put the Kettle On

1. Use **capital letters** where necessary to write the titles below.

   a) my side of the mountain _____

   b) if you're happy and you know it _____

   c) the boy who cried wolf _____

   d) the cat in the hat _____

   e) a wrinkle in time _____

   f) down by the bay _____

2. Write the titles of **one book** and **one movie** you like. Do not choose a title that already appears on this page. Use capital letters where necessary.

   a) book: _____

   b) movie: _____

Who's or Whose?

Use **who's** as the contraction of **who is**.

Example: Who is going to take out the garbage?
Who's going to take out the garbage?

You can also use **who's** as the contraction of **who has**.

Example: Who has left the front door open?
Who's left the front door open?

Use **whose** in questions to find out which person or people **something belongs to**.

Example: Whose purple scarf is this?

You can also use **whose** when you are describing a person or a group of people by talking about **something that belongs to them**.

Example: The man whose house burned down is very upset.

The words **whose house burned down** describe which man you are talking about.

1. Circle the words in brackets that **who's** stands for in each sentence.

   a) Who's going to volunteer to clean up after the party? (who is   who has)

   b) Who's already seen this movie? (who is   who has)

   c) I know who's been leaving the window open. (who is   who has)

   d) That is the girl who's going to sing in the talent show. (who is   who has)

   e) Who's the man standing beside the fountain? (who is   who has)

   f) She asked, "Who's been stealing tomatoes from my garden?" (who is   who has)

   g) I'm not sure who's making all that noise. (who is   who has)

   h) Who's taken the scissors from the kitchen drawer? (who is   who has)

Who's or Whose? (continued)

2. Use **whose** to rewrite each pair of sentences as one sentence. Look at the example below.

Example: The boy's bike was stolen. He lives next door to me.
The boy whose bike was stolen lives next door to me.

a) The writer's book won a prize. She is here today.

_____

b) The man's leg was broken. He walked with crutches.

_____

3. Write **who's** or **whose** to correctly complete each sentence.

a) _____ notebook is this?

b) Do you know _____ car is parked outside?

c) _____ coming to the park with us?

d) The man _____ wallet I found lives near me.

e) She wonders _____ been throwing litter in her yard.

f) I don't know _____ responsible for this mess.

g) _____ eaten at the new restaurant on Oak Street?

h) I felt sorry for the man _____ hat fell into a puddle.

i) Watch the hockey player _____ skating toward the net.

j) Kim is the girl _____ mother works with my father.

k) _____ taken the red marker I left on the table?

Write the Correct Word

Don't be confused by the words below. Check your writing to make sure you have written the right words.

Word	Definition and Example
all ready	completely prepared *Example: I had packed my suitcase, and I was **all ready** for the trip.*
already	before now or before a specific time *Example: I have **already** finished my homework.*
desert	a dry area of land, often covered with sand *Example: The explorer walked across the hot **desert**.*
dessert	sweet food eaten at the end of a meal *Example: We ate spaghetti, and then we had ice cream for **dessert**.*
it's	the contraction for the words *it is* or *it has* *Examples: **It's** time to go now. **It's** been sunny all week.*
its	a possessive pronoun that means **belonging to it** *Example: The squirrel sat up on **its** hind legs.*

1. In each sentence, circle the **correct choice** in the brackets.

a) The airplane made an emergency landing in the (desert dessert).

b) Swimming is fun, and (it's its) a great way to get exercise.

c) I called her house, but she had (all ready   already) left for school.

d) My favourite (desert dessert) is chocolate pudding.

e) I had studied my notes carefully, so I was (all ready   already) for the test.

f) The bus might be late because (it's its) been snowing all morning.

g) Have you (all ready   already) seen this movie?

h) The wagon was missing one of (it's its) wheels.

Canadian Grammar Practice 5 © Chalkboard Publishing

Write the Correct Word (continued)

Make sure you use these words correctly in your writing.

Word	Definition and Example
hole	a hollow place in the ground or the surface of an object *Example: My dog chewed a **hole** in my sock.*
whole	all of something *Example: I read the **whole** book in just two days.*
peace	a state of calm and quiet, without any fighting *Example: She likes the library because she can read in **peace** there.*
piece	a part of something *Example: We found a **piece** of the puzzle under the table.*
threw	past tense of the verb ***to throw*** *Example: I **threw** the football to my teammate.*
through	in one side and out the other *Example: The carpenter drilled a hole **through** the board.*

2. Circle the **correct choice** in the brackets.

a) Soon the war will be over, and we can live in (peace piece).

b) I (threw through) the baseball, and it crashed (threw through) the window.

c) The dime fell (threw through) a (hole whole) in my pocket.

d) I can't eat the (hole whole) pie, but I will have a (peace piece).

e) He crumpled up the page, and then he (threw through) it in the garbage.

f) This (peace piece) of the model airplane fits into that tiny (hole whole).

g) There is no (peace piece) in this house because the dog is always barking.

h) We had good weather the (hole whole) time we were in Halifax.

Word	Definition and Example
stair	a step in a set of stairs *Example: My dog lied down on the **stair** and wouldn't let me past.*
stare	to look blankly, or with eyes fixed in one place and wide open *Example: Our cat can sit and **stare** at the goldfish for hours.*
heel	the back part of a foot or shoe below the ankle *Example: The **heel** fell off the woman's shoe as she ran for the bus.*
heal	to make well or healthy again *Example: John said it would take six weeks to **heal** his broken arm.*
allowed	to be given or to give permission to do something *Example: I'm **allowed** to go to the park, but only if I'm with a friend.*
aloud	in a voice that can be easily heard; not silently or in a whisper *Example: The coach read **aloud** the names of the team members.*

3. Circle the **correct choice** in the brackets.

a) At the memorial, the mayor read (aloud allowed) the fallen soldiers' names.

b) My brother and I play at who can (stair stare) the longest without blinking.

c) The tree was badly damaged by the storm, but Dad says it will (heel heal).

d) Mom (aloud allowed) me and Kathy to play dressup with her clothes.

e) Marty left a toy truck on the (stair stare) and I hurt my foot on it.

f) Our puppy nipped at my (heel heal) when I walked in front of him.

g) A hawk will (stair stare) at the grass to spot a mouse moving through it.

h) When the teacher pointed to us, we had to say a number (aloud allowed).

Correcting Errors: *Editorial*

Find and correct **20 errors** in this editorial.

1   I think that giving students to much homework is a real problem. A little homework each
night is fine but sometimes we get too much!

2   Students need time to play outdoors. Adults say "Young people need to get more
exercise. How are we supposed to get exercise if we spend the hole evening doing
homework.

3   I play on a baseball team. Sometimes, I realize there is a practice or a game on a
night when I had lots of homework. Then no time to relax. Everyone needs some piece
and quiet once in a while.

4   Sports aren't the only thing that keeps students busy after school. Sometimes, I
have to walk the dog help my younger brother with his homework and clean my room.
There is not much time left for my homework. "Have fun while you're young" my mother
says, "Because there is less time for fun when you grow up. I would have more time for
fun if I didn't have so much homework!

5   Too much homework is a problem but homework that is too hard is a worst
problem. Its frustrating when you cant figure out how to do the homework. Teachers
needed to make sure that the homework isn't too hard.

6   I know that homework is important because it gives us a chance to practice what
we learn in school. I think we shouldn't get too much homework, it shouldn't be too
hard.

Correcting Errors: *Crosswords and Tea*

Find and correct **28 errors** in this story.

1   Dad and I had just arrived for a visit with Grandma. She loves doing crossword puzzles and she was showing us her new book of puzzles.

2   "Its called *The big Book Of Amazing Crosswords*," Grandma said. "The first puzzle is hard but I've almost finished it. I just need one more word. It's a name for a beard, and it has six letters. The word starts with *G*."

3   Neither Dad or I could think of the word. "How about some tea?" Dad asked. "Lisa and I will make tea and a snack while you finish off that puzzle."

4   Dad and me went to the kitchen. Dad put the kettle on and I opened a cupboard. Grandma loves herbal teas, and she had a hole shelf full of teas with names like Sleep Tea Energy Tea and Tangy Tea.

5   "What type of tea do you think Grandma wants," I asked Dad.

6   Before he could answer, we heard Grandma call out in a loud voice, "Go Tea!"

7   "I guess she really wants Go Tea," I said. I searched through all the boxes of tea, but there wasn't one called Go Tea.

8   "Maybe she forgot that she ran out of Go Tea," said Dad. "Tangy Tea sounds good, but let's make that instead. See if you can find some crackers and cheese to have with the tea."

9   "Dad she sounds really excited about Go Tea" I replied. "See if you can find any Go Tea."

continued next page

    Canadian Grammar Practice 5 © Chalkboard Publishing

0   Dad looked threw all the boxes of tea on the shelf. Even looked in the other cupboards. He couldn't find Go Tea anywhere so he decided to make Tangy Tea.

1   Dad made the tea while I start to work on crackers and cheese. I carefully cut a peace of cheese to put on each cracker. When the tea and crackers were already, Dad put the teapot, three cups and the crackers on a tray. Then he carried the tray into the living room.

2   "It looks as though you're out of Go Tea," I explained to Grandma, "So we made Tangy Tea. I hope that's okay."

3   Grandma looked confused for a moment, and then she burst out laughing. Dad and me looked at each other with puzzled expressions on our faces.

4   "Grandma what's so funny?" I ask.

5   "I wasn't asking for Go Tea," she explained. "I was just excited that I found the word I was looking for? A *goatee* is a small, pointy beard. The word has six letters and starts with the letter *G*. I finally finished the first crossword puzzle!"

Vocabulary List 1

---

consequence

(noun) something that happens as a result of something else
*Example: Getting cavities is a **consequence** of not brushing your teeth.*

---

terrain

(noun) a particular type of land
*Example: Many animals and insects live in the marshy **terrain** around the pond.*

---

initial

(noun) the first letter of a name
*The note was signed with the **initial** "J," so Julie or Jeff might have written it.*

(adjective) first, or happening at the beginning of something
*Example: The **initial** draft of the story was much longer than the final draft.*

---

astound

(verb) to shock or surprise
*Example: I am sure the magician's amazing tricks will **astound** you.*

---

convey

(verb) to communicate something, such as information, an idea, or a feeling
*Example: Writing a letter to the editor is one way people can **convey** their opinions to a
        wide audience.*

---

ineffective

(adjective) not creating the result or effect that is wanted
*Example: The medicine was **ineffective**, so the patient's illness did not improve.*

---

baffle

(verb) to make someone confused or unable to understand
*Example: My sister is always very polite, so her rude behaviour yesterday **baffled** us.*

Vocabulary List 1 (continued)

In each sentence, write the **correct word** from the vocabulary list. For **verbs**, remember to use the correct form (singular or plural) and tense (past, present, or future).

a) I have some incredible news that is going to _____ you.

b) When sending messages to each other, the spies used a secret code that has

_____ everyone who tried to break it.

c) Going to jail is one possible _____ of breaking the law.

d) The _____ step in building a swimming pool is to dig a large hole in the ground.

e) The _____ in this area is too rocky for farming.

f) The spray we used to kill dandelions was _____, so now our lawn is covered with dandelions.

g) Mrs. Santos sent us a thank-you card to _____ her appreciation for the help we gave her.

h) Helena wrote her _____ on her lunch bag so her sister wouldn't take it by mistake.

i) We knew the restaurant would be expensive, but the prices on the menu

_____ us.

j) Mike said he was afraid of heights, so his decision to go mountain climbing

_____ everyone who knew him.

k) The protesters _____ their anger by shouting at the police.

Write your own sentences using the vocabulary words. Each sentence should clearly show the meaning of a vocabulary word.

Vocabulary List 1: Review

consequence terrain initial astound convey ineffective baffle

1. Write the **correct** vocabulary word beside each definition. You may need to use some words more than once.

a) _____: to make someone confused or unable to understand

b) _____: the first letter of a name

c) _____: something that happens as a result of something else

d) _____: to shock or surprise

e) _____: not creating the result or effect that is wanted

f) _____: first or happening at the beginning of something

g) _____: a particular type of land

2. Write the **correct** vocabulary word in each sentence. For **verbs**, remember to use the correct form (singular or plural) and tense (past, present, or future).

a) Our _____ attempt was not successful, but eventually we did manage to climb to the top of the mountain.

b) I will give a short speech to _____ my thanks to everyone who helped us raise money for the hospital.

c) Leo said he was not very good at crossword puzzles because the clues always

_____ him.

d) It is wise to wear hiking boots when you are going to be walking through rocky

_____.

e) The cut on her head was a _____ of not wearing a bicycle helmet.

f) The scientist's remarkable discovery _____ everyone.

Vocabulary List 2

---

adage

(*noun*) a short, well-known statement that expresses a general truth
*Example: Sometimes when I sleep late, my grandmother repeats the **adage**, "The early bird catches the worm."*

---

endurance

(*noun*) the ability or strength to do something difficult for a long time
*Example: Runners in the marathon will need lots of **endurance** to complete the long race in this hot summer weather.*

---

detect

(*verb*) to discover or notice something that is not obvious
*Example: A dog can **detect** smells that humans would never notice.*

---

excavate

(*verb*) to uncover something that is buried in soil, or to make a hole by digging
*Example: Workers will **excavate** in the backyard, so they can replace the broken underground pipes.*

---

consult

(*verb*) to get information or advice from someone, or to look for information in a source such as a book
*Example: Whenever I am not sure how to spell a word, I **consult** a dictionary to find the correct spelling.*

---

absurd

(*adjective*) very silly or foolish, or not making any sense
*Example: It is **absurd** to believe that the moon is made of cheese.*

---

stern

(*adjective*) serious, strict, or showing disapproval
*Example: The principal gave us a **stern** warning that she would not put up with bullying.*

Vocabulary List 2 (continued)

In each sentence, write the **correct word** from vocabulary list. For **verbs**, remember to use the correct form (singular or plural) and tense (past, present, or future).

a) We got lost when we were in Paris, so we _____ a map to find the way back to our hotel.

b) After hiking all day, I didn't have the _____ to go any farther.

c) "You can't judge a book by its cover" is an _____ that reminds us not to judge people only by their appearance.

d) I could tell by Dad's _____ tone of voice that he wasn't joking.

e) Gary thought it was _____ to take a taxi to the restaurant when it was only a short walk away.

f) The professor _____ an ancient statue from a farmer's field near Rome, Italy.

g) The scientist did several tests to see if they could _____ harmful chemicals in the city's drinking water.

h) When the librarian looked over at us with a _____ expression on his face, we realized we were making too much noise.

i) Before I bought a new computer, I _____ computer reviews on the Internet.

j) The construction workers will need to _____ before they can start building the foundation of the new house.

k) The circus clown made all the children laugh by doing things that were

_____.

Write your own sentences using the vocabulary words. Each sentence should clearly show the meaning of a vocabulary word.

Vocabulary List 2: Review

adage   endurance   detect   excavate   consult   absurd   stern

1. Write the **correct** vocabulary word beside each definition. You may need to use some words more than once.

   a) _____: to get information or advice from someone

   b) _____: a well-known statement that expresses a general truth

   c) _____: to discover or notice something that is not obvious

   d) _____: to make a hole by digging

   e) _____: serious, strict, or showing disapproval

   f) _____: the ability to do something difficult for a long time

   g) _____: very silly or foolish, or not making any sense

   h) _____: to uncover something that is buried in soil

2. Write the **correct** vocabulary word in each sentence. For **verbs**, remember to use the correct form (singular or plural) and tense (past, present, or future).

   a) The _____ expression on the principal's face told us that he was not in a good mood.

   b) If my cough does not get better soon, I will _____ a doctor.

   c) The _____ "Practice makes perfect" encourages us to keep working at improving our skills.

   d) Police officers sometimes use dogs to _____ illegal drugs hidden in packages and suitcases.

   e) It was lucky the woman had enough _____ to swim all the way to shore after her sailboat sank.

   f) The words "ridiculous" and "_____" are synonyms.

Vocabulary List 3

autograph

(*noun*) a signature, usually of someone famous
*Example: His **autograph** was so messy that no one could read his name.*

(*verb*) to write a signature; usually done by someone famous
*Example: The opera singer is going to **autograph** photos of herself to hand out to fans.*

opportunity

(*noun*) a situation or period of time when it is possible to do something
*Example: He left the gate open, which gave the dog an **opportunity** to escape from the yard.*

barrier

(*noun*) a physical object that blocks the way or keeps things apart, or anything that makes it difficult to achieve a goal or make progress
*Example: The police put up a **barrier** to keep cars off the bridge while workers repair it.*

retain

(*verb*) to keep something, or to absorb and hold something (such as heat or water)
*Example: After you sign the forms, please send one copy to me and **retain** the other copy for your records.*

immense

(*adjective*) very large in size or amount
*Example: The cruise ship was so **immense** that people sometimes got lost on it.*

feeble

(*adjective*) weak, or not convincing
*Example: During his long illness, the man was too **feeble** to get out of bed.*

enhance

(*verb*) to increase or improve something
*Example: Studying for a test will **enhance** your chances of getting a good mark.*

 Canadian Grammar Practice 5 © Chalkboard Publishing

In each sentence, write the **correct word** from vocabulary list. For **verbs**, remember to use the correct form (singular or plural) and tense (past, present, or future).

a) The teacher did not believe Tara's _____ excuse for why she was late handing in her assignment.

b) Not being able to speak English can be a _____ to getting a good job.

c) The famous hockey player took a moment to sign his _____ for a young fan.

d) The children learned that a wet sponge is heavier than a dry sponge because a wet

   sponge _____ water.

e) I don't have to get up for school tomorrow, so I'll have an _____ to sleep in.

f) Planting some flowers will _____ the beauty of the backyard.

g) An _____ desert covers most of the continent.

h) The man made a _____ attempt to look happy, but everyone could tell that he was still feeling sad.

i) Mom put up a _____ that will keep the dog from going into the living room.

j) Doing volunteer work at the hospital _____ Verna's reputation as a person who cares about others.

k) The sidewalk was still warm after sunset because the concrete slabs had

   _____ heat from the daytime sun.

Write your own sentences using the vocabulary words. Each sentence should clearly show the meaning of a vocabulary word.

Vocabulary List 3: Review

autograph   opportunity   barrier   retain   immense   feeble   enhance

1. Write the **correct** vocabulary word beside each definition. You may need to use some words more than once.

a) _____: anything that makes it difficult to achieve a goal

b) _____: to increase or improve something

c) _____: a signature, usually of someone famous

d) _____: to keep something

e) _____: weak, or not convincing

f) _____: very large in size or amount

g) _____: a situation or period of time when it is possible to do something

h) _____: a physical object that blocks the way

2. Write the **correct** vocabulary word in each sentence. For **verbs**, remember to use the correct form (singular or plural) and tense (past, present, or future).

a) The explorer wanted to reach the ocean, but the tall mountains were a

_____ that slowed him down.

b) A _____ excuse is an excuse that no one believes.

c) We use a barrel to _____ rainwater for watering our garden.

d) The _____ creature that swam near our ship was a whale.

e) I've been so busy that I haven't had an _____ to visit you.

f) They planted more flowers to _____ the beauty of the park.

Canadian Grammar Practice 5 © Chalkboard Publishing

Vocabulary List 4

strategy

(*noun*) a plan for achieving a goal
*Example: My **strategy** for improving my marks includes not falling asleep in class.*

survey

(*noun*) one or more questions which a large number of people are asked to answer
*Example: We took a **survey** to find out how many students in our school have pets.*

(*verb*) to gather information by asking many people to answer one or more questions
*Example: The company **surveys** people to find out which dish detergent they like best.*

imply

(*verb*) to suggest something without clearly saying it
*Example: The other driver didn't actually blame Mr. Forchuk for the accident, but she **implied** that it was his fault.*

infer

(*verb*) to form an opinion or conclusion based on evidence
*Example: Carmela has been yawning all morning, so I **infer** that she did not sleep well last night.*

numerous

(*adjective*) made up of a large number of something
*Example: The police have received **numerous** complaints about all the graffiti on buildings.*

envious

(*adjective*) wanting to have what someone else has
*Example: Darrell is **envious** of his brother's new bicycle.*

obsolete

(*adjective*) no longer used, often because there is something newer and better
*Example: Fire-burning stoves became **obsolete** after electric stoves were invented.*

Vocabulary List 4 (continued)

In each sentence, write the **correct word** from vocabulary list. For **verbs**, remember to use the correct form (singular or plural) and tense (past, present, or future).

a) The customer did not say that I lied to him, but he _____ it.

b) Printers that make scans are making photocopiers _____.

c) Her _____ for winning the tennis game was to tire out the other player.

d) The teacher _____ the students to find out which math topics they found most challenging.

e) From the handwriting in the letter, I was able to _____ that the writer was a woman.

f) On hot summer days, we are _____ of our neighbour's swimming pool.

g) The bus is almost empty because _____ people got off at the last stop.

h) All of the questions on the _____ asked about activities people do in their spare time.

i) Dad said he wasn't angry at me, but he _____ that I had disappointed him.

j) When writing a test, a good _____ for doing well is to answer the easiest questions first.

k) The mall is very large and contains _____ stores that sell clothing for children.

l) I can _____ from her tone of voice that she is angry.

Write your own sentences using the vocabulary words. Each sentence should clearly show the meaning of a vocabulary word.

Canadian Grammar Practice 5 © Chalkboard Publishing

Vocabulary List 4: Review

strategy   survey   imply   infer   numerous   envious   obsolete

1. Write the **correct** vocabulary word beside each definition. You may need to use some words more than once.

a) _____: wanting to have what someone else has

b) _____: no longer used because there is something better

c) _____: to suggest something without clearly saying it

d) _____: questions a large number of people are asked to answer

e) _____: a plan for achieving a goal

f) _____: made up of a large number of something

g) _____: to form an opinion or conclusion based on evidence

h) _____: to gather information by asking many people questions

2. Write the **correct** vocabulary word in each sentence. For **verbs**, remember to use the correct form (singular or plural) and tense (past, present, or future).

a) Information from the _____ shows that most people like the new mayor.

b) I can _____ your mood from the expression on your face.

c) He had _____ cuts and scrapes after he fell off his bike.

d) Our coach is working on a _____ to help our team win.

e) Don't feel _____ of people who have things you don't.

f) The woman _____ that she was rich, but she never said so.

g) The horse and carriage became _____ soon after cars were invented.

Vocabulary List 5

---

aroma

(*noun*) a distinctive, usually pleasant smell
*Example: The **aroma** of fresh-baked bread greeted Jenny as she walked in the door.*

---

purchase

(*noun*) something that has been bought
*Example: Grandma left the grocery store with her **purchases** packed in two reusable bags.*

(*verb*) to buy something
*Example: Nick had just enough money to **purchase** the book for his brother's birthday.*

---

impressive

(*adjective*) drawing admiration through size, quality, or skill; grand, imposing, or awesome
*Example: She played the piano concerto so **impressively**, the whole audience stood up and clapped.*

---

companion

(*noun*) a person or animal someone spends a lot of time with, or travels with
*Example: My uncle's dog is a great **companion** for him when he feels lonely.*

---

edible

(*adjective*) fit to be eaten
*Example: Nightshade is a plant with red berries that are poisonous, so they are not **edible**.*

---

evade

(*verb*) to escape or avoid, especially by being clever or tricky

---

Canadian Grammar Practice 5 © Chalkboard Publishing

In each sentence, write the **correct** word from vocabulary list. For **verbs**, remember to use the correct form (singular or plural) and tense (past, present, or future).

a) "Wow, Kate," said Uncle Henry, "you have an _____ collection of beautiful seashells!"

b) The stray dog knew every escape route, so he managed to _____ the rescuers for hours.

c) My cat lies in my mother's garden and enjoys the _____ of the catnip around him.

d) Rani went to the lunch counter to _____ an apple for her lunch.

e) The trail guide warned us that the shiny black berries were not _____.

f) My goldfish was alone in the fish tank, so I bought a guppy to be his _____.

g) Marty bought a new painting, and proudly hung his _____ on his bedroom wall.

h) The thief ran through alleys and yards, and managed to _____ police for a few blocks.

i) Todd, Erik, and I used all of our blocks to build a very tall and _____ tower.

j) Cari saw real flowers on the cake, and was surprised to learn that those flowers are

   _____.

k) The tiny cat, the noisy duck, and the huge horse are unusual _____.

l) The woman's hair was down to her knees, which was an _____ length.

Vocabulary List 5: Review

aroma   purchase   impressive   companion   edible   evade

1. Write the **correct** vocabulary word beside each definition. You may need to use some words more than once.

   a) _____: a person or animal someone travels with

   b) _____: to buy something

   c) _____: a distinctive, usually pleasant smell

   d) _____: to escape or avoid

   e) _____: something that has been bought

   f) _____: fit to be eaten

   g) _____: drawing admiration through size, quality, or skill

2. Write the **correct** vocabulary word in each sentence. For **verbs**, remember to use the correct form (singular or plural) and tense (past, present, or future).

   a) With the money I had in my pocket, I _____ a magazine and an orange juice.

   b) Leah wanted to ride the roller coaster, but she needed an adult

   _____ to go on with her.

   c) Dad made cookies for the first time, and he was surprised that they were

   _____.

   d) My favourite scented candle has the _____ of cinnamon rolls.

   e) The woman walked away from the cash register, and left her _____ behind.

   f) Male peacocks have colourful and _____ tail feathers.

   g) My cousin tried to a catch frog, but it managed to _____ her.

Grammar Review Test Grade 5

1. Identify whether the **bold part** of each sentence is the **complete subject** or the **complete predicate**. Circle *CS* for the complete subject or *CP* for the complete predicate.

   a) **The lazy orange cat** slept in my mother's daisies.   *CS   CP*

   b) My sister **painted her toenails very carefully**.   *CS   CP*

   c) **A beautiful rainbow** often follows a heavy rainstorm.   *CS   CP*

   d) After a long work week, **sleeping in on weekends is a great reward**.   *CS   CP*

2. Circle what is missing from the **sentence fragments** below: *CS* for a complete subject, *CP* for complete predicate, or *B* for both.

   a) Dancing in the moonlight.   *CS CP B*

   b) People of all ages.   *CS CP B*

   c) Walk to the library with me?   *CS CP B*

   d) In the corner by the back door.   *CS CP B*

3. Add a **comma** and *and*, *but*, *or*, or *so* to join the two sentences, or **add a period** to separate them.

   a) Mom had a lot of grocery bags to bring in _____ I helped her.

   b) Max could ride his bike _____ Max could play soccer.

   c) I ate a sandwich _____ I drank some milk.

   d) I couldn't find my book _____ Tao had it.

4. Write *CN* beside **common nouns**. Write **proper nouns** with the correct **capital letters**.

a) weekday _____   b) august _____

c) season _____   d) mr. lee _____

e) karen _____   f) labrador _____

g) officer _____   h) calgary _____

5. Write the correct **plural** form for each noun.

a) donkey _____   b) beach _____

c) party _____   d) splash _____

e) weekday _____   f) spiral _____

g) spy _____   h) box _____

6. Circle the correct **possessive noun** in brackets.

a) The purring kitten stopped the (childs' child's) tears.

b) The (firefighter's firefighters') truck was covered in mud after the fire.

c) The (students' student's) test marks were better than they expected.

d) The cupcake (frostings' frosting's) colour was a muddy grey.

7. Underline the **action verbs**. **Do not** underline verbs that **do not** express an action.

a) Sara fell on the sidewalk and scraped her knee.

b) John was very sore after his football game.

c) The frisky baby goat leaped and ran all over the farmyard.

d) The little girl laughed as she threw the fluffy snow in the air.

  Canadian Grammar Practice 5 © Chalkboard Publishing

8. Underline the **verb**. Circle *AV* for an action verb. Circle *LV* for a linking verb.

a) The dog seemed restless before the storm hit.

b) Rain pounded the roof and rushed over the rain gutter.

c) The lightning was bright and the thunder was loud.

d) After the storm, fluffy white clouds skidded across the blue sky.

9. Write the correct **past tense** of the **irregular verb** in brackets.

a) My family _____ a new puppy at the animal shelter. (buy)

b) The workmen _____ a huge hole in the yard to make the pool. (dig)

c) My sister is sick, so she _____ most of the day. (sleep)

d) If I had _____ it was going to rain, I would have brought my umbrella. (know)

10. Look at each **underlined** verb. If the verb tense is **correct**, put a **check mark**. If the verb tense is **incorrect**, write the **correct tense**.

a) Linda is going to the doctor last Wednesday morning. _____

b) My sister gave me a great book for my birthday. _____

c) The light bulb burns out and it was very dark. _____

d) I know all the answers to yesterday's quiz. _____

11. Circle the **antecedent** of the underlined pronoun.

a) Don's foot hurt so badly that he couldn't walk on it.

b) The tree was covered in flowers and bees swarmed all around them.

c) My cousins and I went to the beach, and we had a great time.

d) "Mary, this is the dress you liked, isn't it?" Mom asked.

12. Complete the sentence by writing *I* or *me*.

a) Dari and _____ volunteered to clean the classroom today.

b) Nana gave colouring books to Bekka and _____.

c) Everyone says freckles look nice on _____.

d) When Hans and _____ opened the door, our aunt and uncle came in.

13. Write the correct **demonstrative adjective**: *this*, *that*, *these*, or *those*.

a) I like this pair of shoes a lot, but I prefer _____ on that shelf.

b) Do you want to use this clip in your hair, or would you rather use _____ two?

c) First I dropped my books, then I tripped over _____ chair there.

d) My cat sleeps on that bed sometimes, but he likes _____ bed best.

14. Change the **adjective** in brackets to compare **two things** or **more than two things**.

a) Sam and Dana are _____, but Lars is _____. (funny)

b) Kim is a _____ artist, but Tara is _____ artist in our class. (good)

c) That movie was _____, but this one was _____. (scary)

d) These tiles are all _____, but those are _____. (smooth)

15. Circle the **adverb**. Write whether the adverb describes **how**, **when or how often**, or **where**.

a) Timmy always brushes his teeth before bed. _____

b) Max goes to indoor rock climbing every Thursday afternoon. _____

c) The horse playfully galloped around the field. _____

d) Can we meet outside the theatre? _____

16. Circle the correct word to **compare** two actions or more than two actions.

a) That puppy is (less the least) frisky of the whole litter.

b) Big Charlie is (more the most) woolly than all the other sheep.

c) A true blue rose is (more the most) rare rose of all.

d) After such a long nap, I feel (less the least) tired than I did before.

17. Circle what the **bold adverb** describes: a verb *V*, an adjective *ADJ*, or an adverb *ADV*.

a) Marcel was **extremely** happy he scored a goal in soccer. *V ADJ ADV*

b) The falling meteorite lit up the night sky with a **brilliant** white light. *V ADJ ADV*

c) Jason trudged **sadly** home after losing his favourite ball at school. *V ADJ ADV*

d) Sheila **so** often forgets to put her dirty clothes in the hamper. *V ADJ ADV*

18. Insert **commas** wherever necessary.

a) The marble rolled down the blanket across the rug and out my bedroom door.

b) My baby brother outgrew his shoes so my mother had to buy him a new pair.

c) "Michael did you remember to bring the paper in?" Dad asked.

d) "Your study partner left early did she?" asked Mom.

19. Add quotation marks, periods, commas, and other **punctuation** to this **dialogue**.

a) Enjoy life while you're still young   said my grandfather

b) She just scored the first goal of the season   shouted the commentator

c) I just took my glasses off   said Grandma   but now I can't find them anywhere

d) David do you know where Amir went   asked Jackie

20. Complete the sentence with *either* and *or*, or *neither* and *nor*.

a) I don't like these colours, so I will choose _____ the pink socks _____ the red socks.

b) Tom can _____ ride his skateboard _____ go to his friend's house to play table tennis.

c) Petra has _____ a boy budgie _____ a girl budgie, but she doesn't know which yet.

d) Annie feels very sick this morning, so she wants _____ eggs _____ cereal for breakfast.

21. Rewrite the title with **capital letters**. Remember which words do not get capitals.

a) the old man and the sea _____

b) the farmer in the dell _____

c) up the lazy river _____

d) lucy in the sky with diamonds _____

22. Circle *who's* or *whose* in the brackets. If you pick *who's*, circle which words it stands for.

a) (Who's Whose) coat is lying on the floor here?   who is   who has

b) Do you know (who's whose) coaching our team today?   who is   who has

c) I know (who's whose) left peanut shells on the patio.   who is   who has

d) Guess (who's whose) band is playing on New Year's Eve.   who is   who has

WONDERFUL WORK!

_____
NAME

Achievement Award – Canadian Grammar Practice Grade 5

FANTASTIC GRAMMAR!

_____
NAME

Answers

Types of Sentences, pp. 2–3
(a) exclamation; add exclamation mark (b) question; add question mark (c) statement; add period
(d) exclamation; add exclamation mark (e) command; add period (f) statement; add period (g) question; add question mark (h) command; add period (i) statement; add period

Complete Subjects and Complete Predicates, pp. 4–6
1. Underline the following: (a) The blue car (b) A large black spider (c) The boy with the broken leg (d) Our friends from England (e) The slimy slug (f) Inky black clouds (g) Half the girls in my class (h) A large flock of geese (i) A carton of broken eggs
2. Underline the following: (a) looked at the full moon last night (b) told me about her childhood (c) howled in the distance (d) decided not to finish the marathon (e) drifted gracefully across the pond (f) started drawing and painting when they were children (g) darted in and out of the pond weeds (h) like food better when they help to prepare it
3. Draw a vertical line between the following words: (a) Nancy is (b) fire destroyed (c) team feel (d) friends tried (e) Mabel writes (f) told everyone (g) Ricardo let (h) workers built
4. (a) complete predicate (b) complete subject (c) complete predicate (d) complete subject (e) complete subject (f) complete predicate (g) complete predicate

Avoiding Sentence Fragments, pp. 7–8
1. Circle the following (a) complete subject (b) complete predicate (c) both are missing (d) complete predicate (e) both are missing (f) complete subject
2. (a) CS (b) SF (c) CS (d) SF (e) SF (f) SF (g) CS

Combining Sentences, pp. 9–10
1. (a) Rita washed the dishes, and I put them away. (b) The sky was cloudy, but soon the sun came out. (c) Leave as two sentences (d) I thought Kyle was asleep, but he was awake.
2. (a) I was tired, so I went to bed. (b) Kim might win the race, or she might come in second. (c) I can help you, or you could ask Jeff for help. (d) The sun was shining, so I put on sunscreen. (e) Is Travis coming, or is he still sick? (f) The bus was coming, so I ran to the bus stop.

Correcting Run-On Sentences, pp. 11–12
1. (a) check mark (b) RO (c) RO (d) check mark (e) RO (f) RO
2. (a) I forgot umbrella. I got wet in the rain. / I forgot my umbrella, so I got wet in the rain. (b) My foot slipped on the ice. I didn't fall. / My foot slipped on the ice, but I didn't fall. (c) I might get up early tomorrow. I might sleep in. / I might get up early tomorrow, or I might sleep in.

Sentences Review Quiz, pp. 13–14
1. (a) command; add period (b) question; add question mark (c) statement; add period (d) exclamation; add exclamation mark (e) statement; add period (f) question; add question mark (g) exclamation; add exclamation mark (h) command; add period
2. Draw a vertical line between the following words: (a) garden started (b) Kenji won (c) author writes (d) I took (e) butterfly flew (f) book helps (g) judges awarded (h) ducks lives
3. (a) SF (b) CS (c) SF (d) CS (e) SF (f) SF (g) CS
4. Circle the following: (a) complete subject (b) complete predicate (c) both are missing (d) complete subject (e) both are missing (f) complete predicate
5. (a) Add comma after "charity"; write "so" (b) Add comma after "languages"; write "but" (c) Add comma after "night"; write "or" (d) Add comma after "today"; write "so" (e) Add comma after "cool"; write "and" (f) Add comma after "games"; write "but" (g) Add comma after "night"; write "so" (h) Add a comma after "headache"; write "but"
6. (a) RO (b) check mark (c) RO (d) RO (e) RO (f) RO (g) check mark (h) check mark

Common Nouns and Proper Nouns, p. 16
1. (b) planet (c) street *or* road (d) store *or* business (e) continent (f) ocean (g) country
2. (a) The <u>man</u> took a <u>train</u> to Regina on a rainy <u>day</u>. (b) Did Wendy remember to buy <u>jam</u> at Westside Market?
   (c) My <u>friend</u> said that Neptune is her favourite <u>planet</u>. (d) Sometimes, Uncle Julio sails his <u>boat</u> on Lake Huron.

Exploring Proper Nouns, p. 17
(a) Mr. Chong drove across the Peace Bridge when he visited Hamilton. (b) My grandparents will teach me to speak Russian when they visit next January. (c) On Mother's Day, we visited the Royal Tyrell Museum in Alberta. (d) The Rocky Mountains stretch from Canada to the United States. (e) Some people say English is more difficult to learn than French. (f) Tourists visiting Ottawa often go to see the Parliament Buildings. (g) Students at Lakeview School had a bake sale to help the United Way raise money.

Spelling Plural Nouns, pp. 18–19
1. (a) windows (b) activities (c) lunches (d) brushes (e) monkeys (f) buses (g) taxes (h) journeys (i) eyes
   (j) libraries (k) holidays (l) sixes (m) trays (n) beaches (o) families (p) addresses (q) dishes (r) viruses
   (s) coaches (t) islands (u) berries (v) boxes (w) branches (x) eyelashes
2. (a) videos (b) lives (c) tomatoes (d) pianos (e) thieves (f) roofs (g) wives (h) loaves

Possessive Nouns, pp. 20–21
1. (a) We heard the children's shouts from far away. (b) My neighbours' house is for sale. (c) The tiger's paws had very sharp claws. (d) The birds' chirping woke me up early. (e) Will the students' teacher give them homework? (f) The women's laughter echoed down the hallway.
2. (a) The parrots' frantic screams made everyone cover their ears. (b) The boy's basketball bounced onto our lawn. (c) Cats' claws can badly damage the furniture. (d) The band's instruments sound beautiful when played together. (e) The book's pages are all tattered.
3. Circle the following: (a) Sunset's (b) woman's (c) Horses' (d) team's (e) children's (f) couch's

Nouns Review Quiz, pp. 22–24
1. (a) common (b) proper (c) Proper
2. (b) holiday (c) month (d) street *or* road (e) planet
3. (a) Canadian <u>inventor</u> Alexander Graham Bell invented the <u>telephone</u>. (b) Call Starwell Travel Agency to buy your <u>ticket</u> to Rome. (c) My <u>cousin</u> Jayden is raising <u>money</u> for Toronto General Hospital. (d) Next Monday is Valentine's Day, so my <u>sister</u> is making <u>cards</u> for her <u>friends</u>. (e) Will Mr. Blackwell try to learn Spanish before his <u>trip</u> to Spain? (f) In Ontario, Wasaga Beach is a great <u>place</u> to visit on a hot <u>day</u>. (g) Every <u>year</u>, Labour Day is on the first Monday in September.
4. (a) monkeys (b) peaches, blueberries (c) zeros (d) knives, loaves (e) paragraphs, wishes (f) glasses, boxes
   (g) chefs, tomatoes, potatoes (h) radios, patios (i) photos, videos, heroes (j) trips, wolves (k) wishes, heroes
   (l) flies, dogs (m) fixes, pianos (n) thieves, sheriffs (o) halves, elves (p) roofs, cliffs
5. (a) children's (b) cars' (c) student's (d) men's (e) brother's (f) girls' (g) authors' (h) policemen's (i) butterfly's
   (j) ponies' (k) boys' (l) Ontario's (m) wives' (n) guard's (o) Giraffes' (p) spider's (q) boat's

Action Verbs, p. 25
Underline the following verbs: (a) exploded (b) asked (c) no action verb (d) blew (e) tripped (f) drove (g) no action verb (h) flaps (i) gave (j) told (k) shines (l) no action verb

Linking Verbs, pp. 26–28
1. (a) Circle "excited" and "an adjective." (b) Circle "upset" and "an adjective." (c) Circle "nurse" and "a noun."
   (d) Circle "restless" and "an adjective." (e) Circle "dancer" and "a noun."
2. Underline the following: (a) sounds (b) tastes (c) is (d) become (e) seems (f) became (g) feels (h) smell
3. (a) Underline "are" and circle "LV." (b) Underline "listened" and circle "AV." (c) Underline "were" and circle "LV."
   (d) Underline "is" and circle "LV." (e) Underline "tastes" and circle "LV." (f) Underline "gave" and circle "AV."
   (g) Underline "is" and circle "LV." (h) Underline "became" and circle "LV." (i) Underlined "leaked" and circle "AV."
4. (a) Circle "looks" (b) Underline "talked"; circle "seemed" (c) Circle "feels" (d) Underline "Raking"; circle "is"
   (e) Underline "entered" and "won"; circle "was" (f) Underline "stay" and "leaves"; circle "seems" (g) Underline "left" (h) Underline "whines" and "leave" (i) Underline "say"; circle "is"

The Helping Verbs *Have* and *Has*, p. 29

(a) have washed **(b)** has brushed **(c)** have checked **(d)** has frightened **(e)** have helped **(f)** have glued **(g)** has agreed **(h)** has rained **(i)** have enjoyed **(j)** have decided **(k)** has answered **(l)** have donated **(m)** have eaten

Spelling Past Tense Verbs, pp. 30–31

(a) competed **(b)** tapped **(c)** climbed **(d)** greeted **(e)** studied **(f)** stayed **(g)** fixed **(h)** pinned **(i)** erased **(j)** reached **(k)** jogged **(l)** warned

Past Tense of Irregular Verbs, pp. 32–33

(a) drunk **(b)** brought **(c)** slept **(d)** given **(e)** began **(f)** bitten **(g)** caught **(h)** come **(i)** built **(j)** hidden **(k)** understood **(l)** fed **(m)** been **(n)** eaten **(o)** bent **(p)** driven **(q)** hid **(r)** cut **(s)** known

Using *Should* and *Could*, pp. 34–35

1. (a) could; ability in the past **(b)** should; expected action **(c)** should; advice/suggestion **(d)** could; possibility or might be true **(e)** could; possibility or might be true **(f)** should; expected action **(g)** should; advice/suggestion
2. (a) couldn't **(b)** shouldn't **(c)** couldn't **(d)** shouldn't **(e)** shouldn't **(f)** couldn't
3. (a) should **(b)** couldn't **(c)** shouldn't **(d)** could **(e)** could **(f)** shouldn't **(g)** should **(h)** couldn't

Using the Correct Verb Tense, pp. 36–37

1. (a) will take **(b)** sprained **(c)** am taking **(d)** was walking **(e)** understand **(f)** will be **(g)** sang **(h)** was cutting **(i)** is raining **(j)** watch **(k)** will play **(l)** will stay
2. (a) arrived **(b)** cleaned **(c)** tense is correct **(d)** tense is correct **(e)** says **(f)** will be **(g)** told **(h)** found **(i)** tense is correct **(j)** said **(k)** was **(l)** mowed

Verbs Review Quiz, pp. 38–40

1. (a) Underline "slid" and circle "AV." **(b)** Underline "go" and circle "AV." **(c)** Underline "seems" and circle "LV." **(d)** Underline "were" and circle "LV."
2. (a) Circle "captain" and "a noun." **(b)** Circle "tired" and "an adjective." **(c)** Circle "suspicious" and "an adjective." **(d)** Circle "astronaut" and "a noun." **(e)** Circle "healthy" and "an adjective." **(f)** Circle "librarian" and "a noun." **(g)** Circle "animals" and "a noun." **(h)** Circle "delicious" and "an adjective."
3. (a) have climbed **(b)** has cleaned **(c)** have melted **(d)** has discovered **(e)** has raised **(f)** have baked **(g)** has eaten **(h)** has collected **(i)** has given
4. (a) agreed **(b)** drunk **(c)** sewed **(d)** worried **(e)** eaten **(f)** stayed **(g)** planned **(h)** spent or has spent
5. Circle the following words: **(a)** should **(b)** couldn't **(c)** shouldn't **(d)** could **(e)** could **(f)** should **(g)** should **(h)** could
6. (a) is sleeping **(b)** was walking **(c)** will do **(d)** growls **(e)** watered **(f)** will tell **(g)** researched **(h)** slithered **(i)** will discuss

Pronouns and Antecedents, pp. 41–42

1. (a) She **(b)** them **(c)** us **(d)** We **(e)** they **(f)** I
2. (a) it, them **(b)** He, them **(c)** him, her **(d)** them, they, them
3. (a) Circle "a picture" and draw an arrow from "it" to "a picture." **(b)** Circle "my glasses" and draw an arrow from "them" to "my glasses." **(c)** Circle "My best friend" and draw an arrow from "he" to "My best friend." **(d)** Circle "Tanya" and draw an arrow from "she" to "Tanya"; circle "her watch" and draw an arrow from "it" to "her watch." **(e)** Circle "Many birds" and draw an arrow from "they" to "Many birds"; circle "our birdfeeder" and draw an arrow from "it" to "our birdfeeder." **(f)** Circle "The boys" and draw an arrow from "they" to "The boys"; circle "the concert" and draw an arrow from "it" to "the concert." **(g)** Circle "My parents and I" and draw an arrow from "we" to "My parents and I"; circle "lasagna" and draw an arrow from "it" to "lasagna." **(h)** Circle "Don and Jeff" and draw an arrow from "they" to "Don and Jeff"; circle "Amanda" and draw an arrow from "her" to "Amanda." **(i)** Circle "Juanita and Amit" and draw a line from "us" to "Juanita and Amit." **(j)** Circle "wires and cables" and draw a line from "them" to "wires and cables." **(k)** Circle "my aunt and uncle" and draw a line from "you" to "my aunt and uncle."

Using Pronouns to Avoid Repetition, p. 43

(a) It was so cold that they got out right away. **(b)** She was sure she had heard it before. **(c)** We saw that they were all too green. **(d)** They said they would share them with me. **(e)** She waved at us. **(f)** Please give it back to her.

Choosing Between *I* and *Me*, pp. 44–46

1. (a) I (b) me (c) I (d) I (e) me (f) me (g) I (h) me (i) I (j) me (k) I (l) me
2. (a) me (b) I (c) I (d) me (e) me (f) I (g) me (h) I
3. (a) I (b) me (c) me (d) I (e) I (f) me (g) I (h) me

Possessive Pronouns, pp. 47–48

1. (a) Her cat likes to play, but mine sleeps all day. (b) Our neighbour's house is brown, and ours is white. (c) My pen ran out of ink, so may I use yours? (d) I hung up my coat, but the twins didn't hang up theirs. (e) His store is not very busy, but hers is always busy. (f) We found Leon's baseball cap, but we haven't found mine. (g) The silly goldfish jumped out of its tank again!
2. (a) I thought this book was mine, but it is hers. (b) The dog needed a bath, and its toenails needed trimming. (c) Whose eyes are bluer: mine or his? (d) In the mail, two envelopes were ours and two were theirs. (e) The strong wind caught his umbrella and blew it down the street. (f) This caterpillar is cute. Look at all the fuzz on its body! (g) Most of the class got their tests back already, but I'm still waiting for mine. (h) Our new bedspreads are very pretty. (i) We can't wait to go to Grandma's house to see her new kittens!

Pronoun–Verb Agreement, pp. 49–50

1. (a) comb (b) answers (c) has (d) shout (e) lift (f) hum (g) shows (h) misses, lands (i) borrow (j) have
2. (a) fits (b) arrange (c) helps (d) play (e) fixes (f) has (g) hope (h) blame

Pronouns Review Quiz, pp. 51–53

1. (a) Circle "Alex" and draw an arrow from "You" to "Alex." (b) Circle "The students" and draw an arrow from "they" to "The students." (c) Circle "Yuki and Sonja" and draw an arrow from "they" to "Yuki and Sonja"; circle "jellybeans" and draw an arrow from "them" to "jellybeans." (d) Circle "The boys" and draw an arrow from "they" to "the boys"; circle "some library books" and draw an arrow from "them" to "some library books." (e) Circle "Keisha" and draw an arrow from "she" to "Keisha"; circle "the fossil" and draw an arrow from "it" to "the fossil." (f) Circle "Frank and Joe" and draw an arrow from "they" to "Frank and Joe"; circle "the windows" and draw an arrow from "them" to "the windows." (g) Circle "Angela" and draw an arrow from "she" to "Angela"; circle "the keys" and draw an arrow from "them" to "the keys"; circle "her dad" and draw an arrow from "him" to "her dad." (h) Circle "his hallway" and draw an arrow from "it" to "his hallway."
2. (a) me (b) I (c) I (d) me (e) me (f) I (g) me (h) I (i) me
3. (a) She invited them to the party. (b) They look very nice on them. (c) They ate all of them. (d) She needs to get back to work on it.
4. (a) Your notebook is green, and mine is blue. (b) His cat is white, and theirs is grey. (c) Their team played well, but ours played better. (d) Their house is in the valley, but yours is on the hill.
5. (a) wait (b) misses (c) raises (d) collect (e) crashes (f) show (g) flutters (h) imagine
6. (a) build (b) lends (c) have (d) completes (e) make (f) takes (g) practices (h) follow

Adjectives Before and After Nouns, pp. 54–55

1. (a) Circle "striped" and underline "sweater"; draw an arrow from "striped" to "sweater." (b) Circle "dirty" and underline "clothes"; draw an arrow from "dirty" to "clothes." (c) Circle "long" and underline "movie"; draw an arrow from "long" to "movie." (d) Circle "expensive" and underline "necklace"; draw an arrow from "expensive" to "necklace." (e) Circle "brave" and underline "She"; draw an arrow from "brave" to "She."
2. (a) Circle "dog"; underline "fluffy" (b) Circle "package"; underline "surprise (c) Circle "legs"; underline "long" (d) Circle "thunderstorms"; underline "severe" (e) Circle "lining"; underline "silver" (f) Circle "mud" and underline "slippery"; circle "stream" and underline "shallow" (g) Circle "gowns"; underline "glamorous" (h) Circle "Alice"; underline "nervous"
3. (a) Circle "Fierce," and "ancient"; underline "warriors" and "castle" (b) Circle "old" and "hilarious"; underline "movie" (c) Circle "shiny" and "muddy"; underline "floor" and "boots" (d) Circle "curious" and "new"; underline "We" and "restaurant" (e) Circle "huge"; underline "spider" (f) Circle "long," "sore," and "stiff"; underline "legs" (g) Circle "Red," "white," and "huge"; underline "balloons" and "auditorium"
4. (a) summer (b) silver (c) bravest (d) frightened (e) peaceful (f) morning (g) hungry, thirsty (h) gooey

Adjectives Can Describe How Many, pp. 56–57

1. (a) Circle "several"; underline "sentences" **(b)** Circle "each"; underline "sketches" **(c)** Circle "few"; underline "people" **(d)** Circle "both"; underline "hands" **(e)** Circle "two"; underline "brothers" **(f)** Circle "all"; underline "snakes" **(g)** Circle "Most"; underline "people" **(h)** Circle "Hundreds"; underline "fans" **(i)** Circle "Many"; underline "children" **(j)** Circle "Ten"; underline "bundles" **(k)** Circle "both"; underline "raccoons"

2. Circle the following: **(a)** several **(b)** Some **(c)** Four **(d)** both **(e)** lots **(f)** no **(g)** Every **(h)** dozens

3. Cross out the following: **(a)** Families **(b)** box **(c)** This **(d)** Angry **(e)** brown **(f)** Those **(g)** that **(h)** dirty

Demonstrative Adjectives, p. 58

(a) Those people over by the tree are my friends. **(b)** Will one of these keys in my hand open the lock? **(c)** This box I'm carrying is very heavy. **(d)** Please leave through that door at the end of the hall. **(e)** These socks I'm wearing are very warm. **(f)** That rainbow in the sky is beautiful.

Using Adjectives to Compare, pp. 59–60

1. (a) nicer **(b)** the tallest **(c)** prettier **(d)** hotter, the hottest **(e)** the wisest **(f)** messier, the messiest

2. (a) better **(b)** the best **(c)** farther **(d)** worse **(e)** the most **(f)** the farthest **(g)** more **(h)** the worst **(i)** better

More Ways to Compare with Adjectives, p. 61

(a) more **(b)** the least **(c)** more **(d)** the least **(e)** less **(f)** the most **(g)** less **(h)** the most **(i)** the most **(j)** more **(k)** less **(l)** the least **(m)** the most

Adjectives Review Quiz, pp. 62–63

1. (a) Circle "tall" and draw an arrow from "tall" to "man." **(b)** Circle "sunny" and draw an arrow from "sunny" to "days." **(c)** Circle "Most" and draw an arrow from "Most" to "dogs"; circle "long" and draw an arrow from "long" to "walks." **(d)** Circle "some" and draw an arrow from "some" to "grapes"; circle "yellow" and draw an arrow from "yellow" to "bowl." **(e)** Circle "two" and draw an arrow from "two" to "trees"; circle "huge" and draw an arrow from "huge" to "trees." **(f)** Circle "Several" and draw an arrow from "Several" to "people"; circle "new" and draw an arrow from "new" to "restaurant"; circle "expensive" and draw an arrow from "expensive" to "restaurant." **(g)** Circle "all" and draw an arrow from "all" to "assignments." **(h)** Circle "several" and draw an arrow from "several" to "photos"; circle "interesting" and draw an arrow from "interesting' to "report." **(i)** Circle "All" and draw an arrow from "All" to "children"; circle "unusual" and draw an arrow from "unusual" to "animals."

2. (a) These **(b)** This, that **(c)** That **(d)** These, those **(e)** This, those **(f)** This, that

3. (a) better **(b)** the farthest **(c)** worse **(d)** the most **(e)** the worst **(f)** more *(There are more than two cousins, but the sentence is comparing two things—the number of cousins Lisa has and the number of cousins I have.)* **(g)** the best

4. (a) the most **(b)** less **(c)** more **(d)** the most **(e)** the least **(f)** more

Adverbs Can Describe How, p. 64

1. (a) Circle "quietly" and "peacefully"; underline "spoke" and "slept" **(b)** Circle "gently" and underline "laid"; draw an arrow from "gently" to "laid." Circle "silently" and underline "left"; draw an arrow from "silently" to "left." **(c)** Circle "clumsily" and underline "dropped"; draw an arrow from "clumsily" to "dropped." Circle "noisily" and underline "shattered"; draw an arrow from "noisily" to "shattered." **(d)** Circle "violently" and "unexpectedly"; underline "erupted"; draw arrows from "violently" and "unexpectedly" to "erupted."

2. Circle the following: **(a)** Yes **(b)** No **(c)** Yes **(d)** Yes **(e)** No

Adverbs Can Describe When or How Often, p. 65

(a) when **(b)** how often **(c)** how often **(d)** when **(e)** when **(f)** how often **(g)** when, when **(h)** how often **(i)** when **(j)** how often **(k)** how often **(l)** when, how often **(m)** how often, how often **(n)** when, when

Adverbs Can Describe Where, p. 66

1. Circle the following: **(a)** here **(b)** nearby **(c)** everywhere **(d)** downstairs **(e)** somewhere **(f)** there

2. Circle the following: **(a)** backward **(b)** south **(c)** forward **(d)** up **(e)** left, right, left

Exploring Adverbs That Compare, pp. 67–68

1. (a) the highest **(b)** slower **(c)** brighter **(d)** the loudest **(e)** the slowest **(f)** faster **(g)** higher **(h)** earlier **(i)** the earliest
2. (a) farther **(b)** better, the best **(c)** worse **(d)** the most **(e)** the farthest **(f)** the least **(g)** more **(h)** less

Comparing with *More, Most, Less,* and *Least,* p. 69

(a) more **(b)** less **(c)** the most **(d)** the most **(e)** less **(f)** the least **(g)** more **(h)** the most **(i)** the most **(j)** the least

Adverbs Can Describe Verbs, Adjectives, and Adverbs, pp. 70–71

1. (a) Circle "slightly" and draw an arrow to "annoyed." **(b)** Circle "badly" and draw an arrow to "damaged."
  (c) Circle "incredibly" and draw an arrow to "huge." **(d)** Circle "quite" and draw an arrow to "interested."
  (e) Circle "so" and draw an arrow to "helpful." **(f)** Circle "awfully" and draw an arrow to "cold." **(g)** Circle "really"
  and draw an arrow to "scary." **(h)** Circle "too" and draw an arrow to "hot."
2. (a) verb **(b)** adjective **(c)** verb **(d)** adverb **(e)** adjective **(f)** adverb **(g)** adverb
3. (a) adjective **(b)** adverb **(c)** adverb **(d)** adjective **(e)** adjective **(f)** adjective **(g)** adverb **(h)** adverb **(i)** adjective
  (j) adverb

Adverbs Review Quiz, pp. 72–73

1. (a) Circle "usually" and draw an arrow to "arrives"; circle "sometimes" and draw an arrow to "comes."
  (b) Circle "soon" and draw an arrow from "soon" to "stopped"; circle "outside" and draw an arrow from "outside"
  to "played." **(c)** Circle "so" and draw an arrow from "so" to "loud." **(d)** Circle "before" and draw an arrow to
  "met." **(e)** Circle "straight" and draw an arrow from "straight" to "go." **(f)** Circle "well" and draw an arrow from
  "well" to "sleep"; circle "loudly" and draw an arrow from "loudly" to "snoring." **(g)** Circle "now" and draw an arrow
  from "now" to "leave"; circle "early" and draw an arrow from "early" to "arrive." **(h)** Circle "slowly" and draw an
  arrow from "slowly" to "melted"; circle "brightly" and draw an arrow from "brightly" to "shone." **(i)** Circle "hard"
  and draw an arrow from "hard" to "studied"; circle "quickly" and draw an arrow from "quickly" to "completed."
2. (a) adjective, certain; verb, tell **(b)** verb, ate; adjective, hungry **(c)** adverb, quickly
3. (a) faster **(b)** the earliest **(c)** farther **(d)** the loudest **(e)** the least **(f)** better **(g)** the least
4. (a) more **(b)** the least **(c)** more **(d)** less **(e)** the most **(f)** the least **(g)** the most

Using Commas in Lists, p. 74

1. (a) Joan would like to visit Portugal, Spain, and Italy. **(b)** The American flag is red, white, and blue. **(c)** Harvey,
  Melinda, Frank, and Julio are making signs for the bake sale. **(d)** Wednesday, Thursday, and Friday are busy
  days for me. **(e)** Amy wants to compete in a triathlon race that involves swimming, cycling, and running.
  (f) Mike tries to eat healthy foods such as fruit, vegetables, and grains every day.
2. (a) Dad washed the car, cut the grass, and fed the dog. **(b)** The squirrel ran down the tree, along the fence,
  and across the lawn. **(c)** My sister, my brother, and I searched everywhere for the cat. **(d)** I spend most of my
  time attending school, doing homework, and practicing piano. **(e)** The nurse said that eating nutritious foods,
  drinking lots of water, and getting enough sleep would help me stay healthy. **(f)** I want to finish my homework,
  play a video game, and read my book before bed.

More Ways to Use Commas, p. 75

1. (a) The children went outside to play, didn't they? **(b)** "Terry, you need to listen more carefully," the teacher
  said. **(c)** "Maybe you can come too, John," I suggested. **(d)** No, I haven't yet returned the books to the library.
  (e) Today is Thursday, isn't it? **(f)** Yes, I followed the recipe, but I think I left the cake in the oven too long.
2. (a) No, I haven't done my homework, cleaned my room, or brushed my teeth. **(b)** "Mr. Schwartz, do you speak
  any languages other than English, French, and Spanish?" I asked. **(c)** This coat, hat, and scarf belong to
  Penny, don't they? **(d)** Sal, you set out the utensils, plates, and glasses this morning, didn't you?

Punctuating Dialogue, pp. 76–77

1. (a) "We've won the game!" shouted Chris. **(b)** "I hope we have good weather during our vacation," Dad said.
  (c) "I wonder if she noticed that we came in late," whispered Beth. **(d)** "Would you like to look through the
  telescope?" the scientist asked. **(e)** The coach said, "Now that's what I call teamwork!" **(f)** The crowd shouted,
  "Don't go yet! Sing one more song!" **(g)** My mom said, "I think I've seen this movie before." **(h)** "This produce is
  all organically grown," the woman explained. **(i)** "Tomas, can you come up and write that on the board for us?"
  the teacher asked.

2. (a) "My baby cried most of the night," said Mrs. Hernandez, "and I think it was because she had a fever."
(b) "The woman who lives next door is a doctor," explained Mr. Carson, "but she retired several years ago."
(c) "These red roses are pretty," said the gardener, "but the pink roses are even prettier!" **(d)** "It has been snowing all morning," said Rita, "so I think I'll need to wear my boots when I go outside this afternoon." **(e)** "My parents said you could come to the amusement park with us," said Eddie, "but will you be able to get to my house by noon?"

Punctuation Review Quiz, p. 78

1. (a) "Are you feeling well enough to go to school today?" asked Dad. **(b)** Running, cycling, and swimming are my favourite sports. **(c)** No, we must not allow more animals to become extinct. **(d)** I'll be ready after I get dressed, have breakfast, and brush my teeth. **(e)** You're going to help me with my homework, aren't you?
(f) "Watch out, Maria!" shouted her brother Diego. **(g)** Hamid asked, "Next Monday is Labor Day, isn't it?"
(h) "I might be a while," said Jeff, "so don't wait for me." **(i)** Yes, I'll remember this wonderful day forever.
(j) "You fed the dog, the cat, and the goldfish, right?" asked Tanya.
2. (a) Add a comma after "sister" and circle the comma after the question mark. **(b)** Add a comma after "said"; add a comma after "sweatshirt"; circle the comma after "blouse"; add a period after "dryer." **(c)** Add a quotation mark before "No"; add a comma and then a quotation mark after "restaurant"; circle the quotation mark after "waiter." **(d)** Put a check mark beside the sentence. **(e)** Add a comma after "late"; add a comma between "Lucy" and the quotation mark; circle the comma before "explained"; add a comma after "teacher." **(f)** Add a comma after "Yes"; add a comma after "garbage"; add a comma between "activities" and the quotation mark; add a comma after "Dad."

Using *Either* and *Or*, p. 79

(a) Either Harold or Jane will help me clean up. **(b)** They will either swim or go for a walk. **(c)** Either Cindy or Paul will wash the kitchen floor. **(d)** The woman will either cut her hair or let it grow. **(e)** The children will either play a game or watch a movie.

Using *Neither and Nor*, p. 80

(a) Neither Mom nor Dad could find our hamster. **(b)** The weather was neither windy nor cold. **(c)** The book was neither in my desk nor in my backpack. **(d)** Neither Priya nor Larry could answer the question. **(e)** I was neither sick nor tired.

Using Capital Letters in Titles, p. 81

1. (a) My Side of the Mountain **(b)** If You're Happy and You Know It **(c)** The Boy Who Cried Wolf **(d)** The Cat in the Hat **(e)** A Wrinkle in Time **(f)** Down by the Bay
2. Check that the titles follow the rules for using capital letters in titles.

Who's or *Whose*? pp. 82–83

1. (a) who is **(b)** who has **(c)** who has **(d)** who is **(e)** who is **(f)** who has **(g)** who is **(h)** who has
2. (a) The writer whose book won a prize is here today. **(b)** The man whose leg was broken walked with crutches.
3. (a) Whose **(b)** whose **(c)** Who's **(d)** whose **(e)** who's **(f)** who's **(g)** Who's **(h)** whose **(i)** who's **(j)** whose **(k)** Who's

Write the Correct Word, pp. 84–86

1. (a) desert **(b)** it's **(c)** already **(d)** dessert **(e)** all ready **(f)** it's **(g)** already **(h)** its
2. (a) peace **(b)** threw, through **(c)** through, hole **(d)** whole, piece **(e)** threw **(f)** piece, hole **(g)** peace **(h)** whole
3. (a) aloud **(b)** stare **(c)** heal **(d)** allowed **(e)** stair **(f)** heel **(g)** stare **(h)** aloud

Correcting Errors: *Editorial*, p. 87

Paragraph 1, sentence 1: I think that giving students <u>too</u> much homework is a real problem.
Paragraph 1, sentence 2: A little homework each night is <u>fine</u>, but sometimes we get too much!
Paragraph 2, sentence 2: Adults <u>say</u>, "Young people need to get more exercise.<u>"</u>
Paragraph 2, sentence 3: How are we supposed to get exercise if we spend the <u>whole</u> evening doing homework<u>?</u>
Paragraph 3, sentence 2: Sometimes, I realize there is a practice or a game on a night when I <u>have</u> lots of homework.
Paragraph 3, sentence 3: Then <u>I have</u> [or "there is"] no time to relax.
Paragraph 3, sentence 4: Everyone needs some <u>peace</u> and quiet once in a while.

Paragraph 4, sentence 2: Sometimes, I have to walk the <u>dog</u>, help my younger brother with his <u>homework</u>, and clean my room.

Paragraph 4, sentence 4: "Have fun while you're <u>young</u>," my mother says, "<u>because</u> there is less time for fun when you grow <u>up."</u>

Paragraph 5, sentence 1: Too much homework is a <u>problem</u>, but homework that is too hard is a <u>worse</u> problem.

Paragraph 5, sentence 2: <u>It's</u> frustrating when you <u>can't</u> figure out how to do the homework.

Paragraph 5, sentence 3: Teachers <u>need</u> to make sure that the homework isn't too hard.

Paragraph 6, sentence 2: I think we shouldn't get too much homework, <u>and</u> it shouldn't be too hard.

Correcting Errors: *Crosswords and Tea*, pp. 88–89

Paragraph 1, sentence 2: She loves doing crossword <u>puzzles</u>, and she was showing us her new book of puzzles.

Paragraph 2, sentence 1: "<u>It's</u> called *The Big Book <u>of</u> Amazing Crosswords*," Grandma said.

Paragraph 2, sentence 2: The first puzzle is <u>hard</u>, but I've almost finished it.

Paragraph 2, sentence 3: I just need to figure out <u>one</u> more word.

Paragraph 3, sentence 1: Neither Dad <u>nor</u> I could think of the word.

Paragraph 4, sentence 1: Dad and <u>I</u> went to the kitchen.

Paragraph 4, sentence 2: Dad put the kettle <u>on</u>, and I opened a cupboard.

Paragraph 4, sentence 3: Grandma loves herbal teas, and she had a <u>whole</u> shelf full of teas with names like Sleep <u>Tea</u>, Energy <u>Tea</u>, and Tangy Tea.

Paragraph 5, sentence 1: "What type of tea do you think Grandma wants<u>?</u>" I asked Dad.

Paragraph 8, sentence 2: Tangy Tea sounds good, <u>so</u> let's make that instead.

Paragraph 9, sentence 1: "<u>Dad</u>, she sounds really excited about Go <u>Tea</u>," I replied.

Paragraph 10, sentence 1: Dad looked <u>through</u> all the boxes of tea on the shelf.

Paragraph 10, sentence 2: <u>He</u> even looked in the other cupboards.

Paragraph 10, sentence 3: He couldn't find Go Tea <u>anywhere</u>. so he decided to make Tangy Tea.

Paragraph 11, sentence 1: Dad made the tea while I <u>started</u> to work on crackers and cheese.

Paragraph 11, sentence 2: I carefully cut a <u>piece</u> of cheese to put on each cracker.

Paragraph 11, sentence 3: When the tea and crackers were <u>all ready</u>, Dad put the teapot, three <u>cups,</u> and the crackers on a tray.

Paragraph 12, sentence 1: "It looks as though you're out of Go Tea," I explained to Grandma, "<u>so</u> we made Tangy Tea. ..."

Paragraph 13, sentence 2: Dad and <u>I</u> looked at each other with puzzled expressions on our faces.

Paragraph 14, sentence 1: "<u>Grandma</u>, what's so funny?" I <u>asked</u>.

Paragraph 15, sentence 1: "I wasn't asking for Go Tea," she <u>explained</u>, "I was just excited that I found the word I was looking for! ..."

Vocabulary List 1, pp. 90–91
(a) astound **(b)** baffled **(c)** consequence **(d)** initial **(e)** terrain **(f)** ineffective **(g)** convey **(h)** initial *or* initials
(i) astounded **(j)** baffled **(k)** conveyed

Vocabulary List 1: Review, p. 92
1. (a) baffle **(b)** initial **(c)** consequence **(d)** astound **(e)** ineffective **(f)** initial **(g)** terrain
2. (a) initial **(b)** convey **(c)** baffled **(d)** terrain **(e)** consequence **(f)** astounded

Vocabulary List 2, pp. 93–94
(a) consulted **(b)** endurance **(c)** adage **(d)** stern **(e)** absurd **(f)** excavated **(g)** detect **(h)** stern **(i)** consulted
(j) excavate **(k)** absurd

Vocabulary List 2: Review, p. 95
1. (a) consult **(b)** adage **(c)** detect **(d)** excavate **(e)** stern **(f)** endurance **(g)** absurd **(h)** excavate
2. (a) stern **(b)** consult **(c)** adage **(d)** detect **(e)** endurance **(f)** absurd

Vocabulary List 3, pp. 96–97
(a) feeble **(b)** barrier **(c)** autograph **(d)** retains **(e)** opportunity **(f)** enhance **(g)** immense **(h)** feeble **(i)** barrier
(j) enhanced **(k)** retained

Vocabulary List 3: Review, p. 98

1. (a) barrier (b) enhance (c) autograph (d) retain (e) feeble (f) immense (g) opportunity (h) barrier
2. (a) barrier (b) feeble (c) retain (d) immense (e) opportunity (f) enhance

Vocabulary List 4, pp. 99–100

(a) implied (b) obsolete (c) strategy (d) surveyed (e) infer (f) envious (g) numerous (h) survey (i) implied (j) strategy (k) numerous (l) infer

Vocabulary List 4: Review, p. 101

1. (a) envious (b) obsolete (c) imply (d) survey (e) strategy (f) numerous (g) infer (h) survey
2. (a) survey (b) infer (c) numerous (d) strategy (e) envious (f) implied (g) obsolete

Vocabulary List 5, pp. 102–103

(a) impressive (b) evade (c) aroma (d) purchase (e) edible (f) companion (g) purchase (h) evade (i) impressive (j) edible (k) companions (l) impressive

Vocabulary List 5: Review, p. 104

1. (a) companion (b) purchase (c) aroma (d) evade (e) purchase (f) edible (g) impressive
2. (a) purchased (b) companion (c) edible (d) aroma (e) purchase (f) impressive (g) evade

Grammar Review Test Grade 5, pp. 105–110

1. (a) complete subject (b) complete predicate (c) complete subject (d) complete predicate
2. (a) complete subject (b) complete predicate (c) complete subject (d) both are missing
3. (a) Add a comma and "so"; or add a period (b) Add a comma and "or" (c) Add a comma and "and" (d) Add a period
4. (a) common noun (b) August (c) common noun (d) Mr. Lee (e) Karen (f) Labrador (g) common noun (h) Calgary
5. (a) donkeys (b) beaches (c) parties (d) splashes (e) weekdays (f) spirals (g) spies (h) boxes
6. (a) child's (b) firefighters' (c) students' (d) frosting's
7. Underline the following: (a) fell, scraped (b) no action verbs (c) leaped, ran (d) laughed, threw
8. (a) Underline "seemed"; linking verb (b) Underline "pounded" and "rushed"; action verbs (c) Underline "was"; linking verb (d) Underline "skidded"; action verb
9. (a) bought (b) dug (c) slept (d) known
10. (a) went (b) check mark (c) burned (d) knew
11. Circle the following: (a) Don's foot (b) flowers (c) My cousins and I (d) Mary
12. (a) I (b) me (c) me (d) I
13. (a) those (b) these (c) that (d) this
14. (a) funny, funnier (b) good, the best (c) scary, scarier (d) smooth, smoothest
15. (a) circle "always"; when or how often (b) circle "every Thursday afternoon"; when or how often (c) circle "playfully"; how (d) circle "outside"; where
16. Circle the following: (a) the least (b) more (c) the most (d) less
17. Circle the following: (a) adjective (b) adjective (c) verb (d) adverb
18. (a) The marble rolled down the blanket, across the rug, and out my bedroom door. (b) My baby brother outgrew his shoes, so my mother had to buy him a new pair. (c) "Michael, did you remember to bring the paper in?" Dad asked. (d) "Your study partner left early, did she?" asked Mom.
19. (a) "Enjoy life while you're still young," said my grandfather. (b) "She just scored the first goal of the season!" shouted the commentator. (c) "I just took my glasses off," said Grandma," but now I can't find them anywhere." (could also end in an exclamation mark) (d) "David, do you know where Amir went?" asked Jackie.
20. (a) neither, nor (b) either, or (c) either, or (d) neither, nor
21. (a) The Old Man and the Sea (b) The Farmer in the Dell (c) Up the Lazy River (d) Lucy in the Sky with Diamonds
22. Circle the following: (a) Whose (b) who's; who is (c) who's; who has (d) whose

Canadian Grammar Practice 5 © Chalkboard Publishing

www.ingramcontent.com/pod-product-compliance
Lightning Source LLC
Chambersburg PA
CBHW081342090426

42737CB00017B/3260